LIOBANI

I Explain - Will You Join Me?

D1726730

LIOBANI
I Explain – Will You Join Me?

THE WORD
THE UNIVERSAL SPIRIT

First Edition, 2010
Published by:
© Universal Life
The Inner Religion
PO Box 3549
Woodbridge, CT 06525
U S A

Licensed edition
translated from the original German title:
"LIOBANI – Ich erkläre – machst Du mit?"
Order No. S 130en

Gabriele Publishing
The Word

www.gabriele-publishing.com

ISBN 978-1-890841-66-9

Fotos:
© Franz Pfluegl - fotolia.com (playing basketball; girl on boulder, background)
© Diego Cervo - fotolia.com (boy playing guitar)

Do you choose the path
of joy and cheer
into old age?

Then accept the spiritual teachings
and guidance
for young people
from twelve to eighteen years of age

revealed by Liobani,
an angel of the Lord,
through our sister Gabriele,
the prophetess and messenger of God

Table of Contents

Introduction

The divine world is very close to those people who daily strive to fulfill the will of God.

This revelation was given for all young people from twelve to eighteen years of age.

Adults who want to keep learning will also find what brings them closer to God in their lives. These truths will also help parents gain more understanding for their growing children – no matter whether they are still in school or have already entered a profession.

The children of this earth grow up; they become young people and adults. Children, the youth and adults should become more and more aware of the fact that they are merely guests on this earth. Every guest on earth should behave as the host – who is God, our Father – wishes from His human children.

God, the law of love, urges a person to think and live as the law, God, the host of love, wishes from His human children – so that they may again enter their heritage of infinity. This heritage is the entire pure cosmic radiation of infinity. Every spirit being is the essence of it. All pure Being is pure cosmic radiation, the law of eternally selfless love.

There is a spiritual body in every person that – as long as it is in a material body – is called a *soul*. The pure spiritual body comes from the pure Being, from God.

Each soul is burdened, that is, shadowed, differently. Thus, the soul in the person is a guest on this earth. It returns to God, its origin, when its burdens, its sins, have been cleared up. Once it is purified, that is, pure again, the pure spiritual body returns to God in the eternal cosmic radiation.

A human being consists of three differently vibrating energies which form a tri-unity. It consists of the incorruptible *spirit,* God, the law of love, of the *soul* and of the physical *body.*

The incorruptible core of Being, the Spirit, God, is enveloped by the spiritual body, the ether body, which with its enveloping garments is called soul. The physical body, that is, the human organism, therefore envelops the soul body. This is why the human being consists of spirit, soul and physical body.

And so, during its journey over this earth, the soul is in a human body. Both soul and person have the task during their journey over this earth – where they are merely guests – to actualize the eternal divine laws and to lead a life that is pleasing to God.

If the guest on earth, the human being, endeavors to fulfill the divine laws, the soul will become pure again and the spirit body will again be the universal Being, that is, the law of love itself. The spirit being, the pure ether body, is again consciously the child, the son or daughter of God.

The one who strives to unfold the laws of God in himself, this means, who lets his spiritual being, the spirit body, shine again, is also surrounded by light-filled, divine forces.

A person's soul can be compared to a great magnet. The soul, the magnet, attracts whatever the person feels, thinks and says. The person's actions are also registered by it, as well as his behavior patterns.

This means that the soul in a human being is the *book of life.* It registers both the positive and the negative. Thus, everything that goes out from a person will enter him again, that is, his soul. And so, all the human aspects that we felt, thought, spoke and did on our journey on earth, and thus, everything that is not forgiven and therefore not erased, remains registered in the soul.

Through good, selfless feelings, thoughts, words and actions, the soul becomes bright. The soul receives light and strength – and the person, the shell of the soul, becomes healthy, happy and glad.

The positive forces shape and mold the person as do the negative forces. The positive forces give rise to a finer physical structure. The person's senses are refined; his whole radiation becomes purer and more beautiful. Even when the physical body withers, its radiation remains youthful because the soul is imbued with light and strength. Although the physical body withers with age – the person retains his youthful freshness.

Whatever is in the soul, light or shadow, radiates through the person's organism and imprints him. External signs of a mature soul, permeated by the light of God, are harmonious gestures, an upright gait, a free and bright face, a balanced manner of speech, in which love and peace vibrate. What and how a person eats, what and how he drinks or the way he dresses – all this indicates whether he is imbued by the light or lives in the shadow of his wrong conduct.

The true life is *within* a person and not outside him. Therefore, from his childhood on, a person should be taught and brought up accordingly, in order to develop this inner life.

Already in earliest childhood, parents should impart to their child why it is on earth and that it consists of the tri-unity: of spirit, soul and body. The child should know the law of sowing and reaping – and know that fate doesn't fall upon us from without, but comes from our very own burdened soul, and that external things merely trigger it. The child should also know about the law of reincarnation; it should know that the soul will continue to enter the flesh until it has dissolved its ties to matter, its wishes and desires. The child should also be taught about the effect of causes not atoned for: The soul will continue to be tied to another soul and can be led together with it until both have cleared up what lay as a burden in their souls – by forgiving, asking for forgiveness, and making amends.

The parents have a large responsibility toward God and their children. It is their duty not only to bring up their children according to the divine laws and to teach them what God, our heavenly Father, wants of them, but both also bear the responsibility – each parent on his own – of being living examples for their children, not only teachers of theory! It is only when the parents themselves have *actualized* what they teach their children that the latter are willing to accept and to follow their parent's advice.

A person who instructs and guides his children out of his own actualization is kind and responsible. He always senses the right moment to tell his child what is essential, wholesome and good for it right then. Parents who direct and guide their children from the treasury of their own actualization are also aware when their child closes its mind to an instruction. And they know how to instruct their child, so that their advice falls into their child's heart, and can be accepted and followed by it.

From the eternal, divine kingdom I, Liobani, now convey the eternal laws, the message of selfless love, and the law of sowing and reaping. For my human brothers and sisters, I call myself Liobani. I am a heavenly sister and convey the eternal truth to all willing people striving toward God, especially the young brothers and sisters from the ages of twelve to eighteen years. However, for people who are older in terms of the laws of nature, the eternal truth can be a deep enrichment for their life on earth.

In Universal Life, Christ's Redeemer-work for all people, the school of Inner Life is taught. It encompasses all seven steps of evolution until perfection, the primordial source, God. Many adults already follow the Inner Path of love to God.

Many an adult finds it very difficult to change his or her way of thinking, to leave the old, beaten tracks, to cast off the old patterns of their human ego and instead to feel, think, speak and act in a lawful way.

We can compare a human being to a so-called computer. When the data, and thus, the programs, have been stored in an elderly person for a long time, it may take quite a lot of time and effort to delete an old program. But for a young person, it is much easier. Although his soul may very well have brought light and shadow into his life on earth, his brain cells are not yet programmed with human patterns of thinking, with old habits and desires.

The young person is like a young tree. He can still bend easily. An elderly person is like an old tree that has been firmly rooted in its place for decades and can no longer be bent; he follows his beaten track that he can leave only with difficulty. This means that in many aspects he finds it very hard to change his way of thinking, to counter his old human patterns with divine thoughts, to ask for forgiveness and to forgive.

However, the love and grace of our heavenly Father in Christ make it possible for *every* human child to break old restrictions and patterns, to give up old habits, to find its way out of human stereotypical thinking patterns and to actualize the divine laws. The Lord of Life can do anything if the person is willing to change his way of thinking. Then he finds his way from human, self-centered thinking to universal thinking

– to love, peace and harmony. Then he also finds the good in every person; for in every unlawfulness, there is a good core.

Dear brother, dear sister, who are still young in earthly years, I give a revelation through a person whom our eternal Lord calls his prophetess and messenger. Through her, He conveys the divine truth, the eternal law, to you.

Please note: I merely *convey* to you the eternal truth and explain how you can attain it. For you should know that God pours His eternal law, the eternal truth, into matter. But, He respects the free will of His children. For this reason, it is up to you whether you accept my explanations and strive to actualize them or whether you reject them.

But if along with many others you walk the selfless path of love, that is, if you join in, all of heaven rejoices. Christ, your Redeemer, is the Good Shepherd. He rejoices over every sheep that finds its way to His flock. And we divine beings rejoice with Him.

Liobani,
a sister from the light

The spiritual body of the children of God – The spiritual atoms of the soul – Every energy has its own color – The field of light of the soul, the aura of a human being

Dear brother, dear sister. It is my wish to be allowed to address you as my brother or my sister.

I am glad that you are happy to accept this term as a greeting from heaven.

In the Spirit of God you are my brother or my sister. In the Kingdom of God we all are brothers and sisters, since we belong to *one* heavenly Father, who is also our Mother. It is the Father-Mother-God, who beheld and created our spiritual body.

We are brothers and sisters – whether you are in the earthly garment, or I am in the spirit garment, that is, not incarnated. In God, we are one. Whether we can or cannot see each other is unimportant. Through the power of God, we are connected, brother and sister.

You must know that for as long as the soul, the spiritual body, is in an earthly garment, it looks through the eyes of the person and often sees only what the person is able to see.

You will wonder about this statement: The soul sees only what the human being is able to see. I would like to explain it more to you:

The spiritual body that is active in your physical body is surrounded by fine, ethereal garments. We also call these garments the *aura* of a person.

In your spiritual body, your soul, everything that you ever felt, thought or said during your former lives on earth and in

17

your present earthly existence is registered. All your actions are registered in your soul. Whatever human aspect you have not yet cleared up radiates now from your soul into your physical body. The person is marked by this; it also has an effect on his senses. Your soul will continue to register everything you feel and think, speak and do for as long as you live on earth as a human being.

The eyes of the soul see light or dark. It totally depends on what light or shadow the person has registered in his soul. The soul looks out through the person; it registers only as much as the person's eyes are able to see and his other senses are able to grasp.

A person's senses are either *guided* by the light of his soul or *controlled* by its burdens. A person sees only according to his light or shadowed sides, according to his thoughts, words and his actions. A kind person finds the good in everything. A negatively polarized person seeks the negative in all things.

Surely you are interested in knowing how the soul is put together and in which way the human body has come into being. You must know that the physical body consists of compact energy. It forms the cells, bones, sinews, muscles, ligaments, glands, vessels and everything that the organism consists of. Compared to the spirit body, the physical body is solid, firm and inflexible.

On the other hand, the spiritual body is a fully flexible structure, having neither bones nor sinews or muscles; nor has it glands or vessels, nor blood or other substances. The spiritual body consists totally of spiritual particles. You can imagine the spiritual particles as being like a honeycomb or the scales of a fish. Layer upon layer, the particles are joined to each other and overlap like the scales of a fish.

I repeat: The spiritual particles are arranged like fish scales. They are positioned in layers. Each layer of particles – also called particle field, particle unit or particle area – contains within itself one great sphere of consciousness of infinity: for example, the sphere of consciousness of the minerals, the plants, the animals, the nature beings, the four spiritual elements of fire, water, earth and air, and finally the entire cosmic event in creation and in the countless pathways of radiation of the eternal homeland. This, all in all, is the law of God.

And so, the particles of the whole spirit body contain all spheres of consciousness of infinity. Each particle field is consciousness of infinity. The whole spirit body thus consists of all the spheres of consciousness of the pure Being, the universal life.

The Spirit of the Father-Mother-God is flowing energy. It is comparable to the air you breathe. It contains many components required by your body. In a similar way, the spirit being is permeated and respirated by the spirit energy, God – and it breathes the breath of God, the flowing energy, God. Your body is sustained by air and food, your spirit body by the energy, God.

Therefore, God's energy breathes throughout the spirit being; it lives on the eternally flowing energy of God, which maintains everything with power and light. On the other hand, on earth everything is maintained by solid matter, for example, by the fruits of the fields and the woods.

The energy, God, the life of the whole, is also called the flowing divine *ether*. The spirit being does not require coarse-material food like the human body does. It lives on the energy of God, the universal ether, which flows throughout all particles and nourishes them.

Let me summarize: For as long as you are a human being, you need the earthly food, the fruits of the fields. The spiritual body, however, is sustained by the universal ether, God.

Now you will wonder what is in the spiritual particles of your spirit body and what these particles are made of.

The spiritual particles themselves and their content consist of countless *spiritual atoms*. The spiritual world consists of spiritual, fine-material energy, of spiritual atoms – just as matter consists of coarse-material energy, of material atoms. All of infinity, all Being, is based on the well-ordered *five spiritual types of atoms.*

In the spiritual atoms, the creation principle is also active. They are the four elementary forces, *Order, Will, Wisdom* and *Earnestness,* the creation and creating energies.

In the center of these cosmic-atomic creation and creating energies, is a mighty energy of pulsation; we could also say an atom in an atom. This mighty energy of pulsation – also called the atom of pulsation – consists of the three forces of filiation. They are *Love,* the strongest power in infinity and in the children of God, and further, the forces of gentleness, also called *Patience,* and *Mercy,* also called kindness and humility.

Those five spiritual types of atoms, which you have heard about, are individually, the *atoms of pulsation,* the *atoms of fertility,* the *carrier atoms,* the *atoms of creation* and the *atoms of development.* All of infinity is made up of these five spiritual types of atoms. In the spirit, as well, everything consists of an atomic structure.

Each spiritual atom in every single particle of the spirit body, as well as in all of infinity, is aligned with the central star of infinity, the *Primordial Central Sun,* and with its *prism suns,* which split the light of the Primordial Central Sun into the lights of the spectrum and radiate into infinity.

The Primordial Central Sun is the Father-Mother-Spirit-Principle, the giving and the receiving principle. Through seven prism suns – also called secondary primordial suns – the Father-Mother-Principle nourishes all of infinity.

And so, material life, too, can exist only through the light of God. All forms of life, for instance, stones, minerals, plants and animals, are forms of consciousness. They receive light and power from the Creator-Spirit according to their state of consciousness.

The state of consciousness can be compared to a bowl. It can hold only according to its size. And so, every single form of life receives light and power only according to its spiritual development, its spiritual size.

The spiritual body of the children of God, which includes your own spiritual body, too, is a mature, that is, a fully developed, spiritual form. Every matured form, that is, every child of God, is in possession of all cosmic powers. These countless fields or powers of consciousness are united as a whole in the spirit child. This means that the child of God, the perfect being, is the divine law.

The spiritual body, and thus, your spiritual being, formed itself via the minerals, plants, animals and nature beings. This did not happen in the material world, but in the spheres of development of God, in the heavens.

Surely, you have read in the revelation "I Give Advice – Will You Accept?" for children from six to twelve years, that a fully mature nature being is raised to the filiation of God and that the maturing child of God gradually fully develops the three attributes of filiation which are Patience, Love and

Mercy, also known as gentleness, love and humility, thus attaining full maturity, that is, it becomes the law of God itself.

And so, when the spirit child is fully developed, then it is respirated by and imbued with the entire primordial energy. All five spiritual types of atoms are fully developed and fully in action. The spiritual particles thus breathe the breath of God.

Once a spirit being is fully developed, then the Father-Mother- Principle is also fully matured in it. It is the spiritual procreative force that comes from the three attributes of filiation.

The four creation powers Order, Will, Wisdom and Earnestness also contain the Father-Mother-Principle, because each spiritual atom contains Patience, Love and Mercy as pulsation energy. However, it is only when the spiritual child has attained full maturity, that is, has become the law of God, that these three powers are fully active.

When in the heavenly worlds a matured nature being is raised to the filiation of God by spiritual procreation, then the Father-Mother-Powers are activated and perfected in it. The matured spirit being can apply all the powers of infinity and create and form from them.

The five spiritual types of atoms are fully active in the matured spirit being and aligned with the primordial power. Therefore, the spirit being radiates all seven basic powers of infinity and can apply them accordingly. Not only does it behold the eternal laws and know the things and events in infinity – it can also move them according to the eternal law, because it has become the law, itself.

The regard of a pure being is not clouded by so-called soul garments, that is, by burdens. It lives in the Absolute and gives from the Absolute, from the eternal law.

How is it with human beings? If in his former lives, which means in the soul's earlier incarnations, and in his present earthly existence a person has violated the divine law and not yet cleared this up, the spiritual atoms of the soul have turned away from the law of God, the primordial power.

Recognize that each sensation, each thought, each word, and each action of the person, positive and therefore lawful, as well as negative and therefore unlawful, causes a reaction in the soul.

So you are quite right to say: Every action – be it positive or negative – is followed by the corresponding reaction.

When a person lives in accordance with the divine law, the spiritual atoms of his soul are aligned with the primordial power. Then the person's soul as well as his body receives much life energy. Then the person beholds things and events as they really are, and not as they appear in the material world.

He also sees right through his fellowmen and knows what they feel and think. And so, he sees how they are, and not how they pretend to be. He sees nature and himself as a whole. He sees every form of life as a part that lives in God and knows that he, too, lives in God as a drop in the ocean, God, the unity.

However, if his thinking and behavior are negative, then the person violates the laws of God. He is then no longer *for* his fellowman, but is against all those whom he finds disagreeable or who do not comply with his will. Through this, he disparages his neighbors; he judges, passes sentence on them and condemns them – thus rejecting them.

But the one who is against his fellowmen, who rejects them, is thus also against God and commits a sin. Through this, the soul's spiritual atoms turn away from the primordial power, the light and the power of God, and turn toward the world. The soul and the person grow poorer in light and strength.

Every burden, that is, every sin, is a violation of the eternal law. This takes effect in the spiritual atoms, which then gradually turn away from the primordial power. The spiritual particles of the soul become shadowed, accordingly – they diminish in light – because they absorb the causes sown by the person.

Your science has recognized that everything is energy and that no energy is lost. So, in feeling, thinking, speaking and acting, a person likewise sets free energies.

If he feels, thinks and speaks selflessly, if he meets his neighbor in a kind and peaceful manner, he develops positive, lawful powers. They strengthen his soul and his body: Soul and person then increasingly receive God's light and power, because the spiritual atoms turn toward the primordial energy. His lawful actions are supported by the eternal law so that whatever the light-filled person carries out in the name of God is successful.

You have heard of the light spectrums that come from God's prism suns. These pure primordial lights are the fine life energies for minerals, plants, animals, nature beings, spirit beings – and for the human being, as well. For him, they are light, power, health and help in every situation. When the person turns away from these pure and fine light spectrums, he burdens himself; the further consequence of this is that he suffers, in the end.

With his wrong behavior, the person creates his own energies, which have their corresponding colors. All sensations, thoughts, words and actions have their specific colors.

Negative sensations, thoughts, words and actions darken the soul particles; thus, these absorb the color of the energies, the vibration, sent out by the person. Light-filled, selfless sensations, thoughts, words and actions of the person brighten the soul particles. The spiritual atoms then turn more and more toward the primordial light, the Primordial Central Sun.

Both, the light as well as the shadow, have an effect on the person's body. Whatever is unlawful not only shadows the soul's particles, but also radiates its color intensity throughout the body. Whatever is registered in the soul's particles, light or shadow, will radiate, in turn, throughout the person and around him.

And so, what a person has sown into the soul particles radiates out; this is then the soul's field of light, the person's aura. It is an ever moving and pulsating energy that radiates various colors.

The law of God consists of the seven basic powers: Order, Will, Wisdom, Earnestness, Patience, Love and Mercy. Since each power is contained in the others, there are seven times seven energetic powers that form the law of God.

If the person has violated this law of God, this will have an effect on his soul and also on his body, for each cause radiates. Through this, as you have already read, the soul's field of light is formed, the person's aura.

Therefore, every person is within *that* particular sphere of light that he has created and is creating himself: Either he stands in the light of God, if he keeps his soul clean for the most part or purifies it by being kind-hearted, loving and understanding, asking forgiveness for all his human aspects and by forgiving, or his aura, his soul's field of light, is dark, from dark red to dark green, dark purple, from gray right down to black.

It is the soul's task to become pure while in the human body, to reduce, with Christ, its Redeemer, its burdens and to lead a peaceable life. Then the soul garments that formed through the violations of the divine law will dissolve and God's life and power will again radiate directly through the soul into and through the person's body. Then the person is beautiful from within, even when the physical body withers. He is attuned to the divine and refined. His language is harmony, and his gestures are noble.

But when the soul garments affect the person's body, then the person also shows himself accordingly. He is envious, spiteful, nagging and quarrelsome. He judges and condemns, is dishonest and self-centered. He constantly expects something from his neighbor; however, he is himself quite reluctant to contribute selflessly.

The soul garments affect all five senses. The person sees and hears only what is in his soul garments, what he is able to see and hear through them. He smells and tastes only what is in his soul garments and what he is able to smell and taste through them. He touches and thus feels only what his soul garments dictate to him.

In this way, people are controlled by their own thought patterns, desires and passions. The person sees, hears, smells, tastes and touches only what lies in himself, what is active in him and takes place in himself. Therefore, how you think, how you behave, that is who you are, yourself:

How do you react when you see something disagreeable?
How do you react when you hear something disagreeable?
How do you react when you smell or taste something disagreeable?
How do you react when you touch something that is disagreeable to you?

I repeat: What you think and how you behave as a consequence of this, that is who you are!

Recognize that selfless, positive thoughts and behavior patterns come from the deep, light-filled areas of your soul. Negative emotions and thoughts and the resulting movements of the body come from the burdened soul, from the shadowed soul particles.

The direct and the indirect guidance of God on the various levels of consciousness – Indirect guidance via events, people, blows of fate and the energy of the day

God is spirit and dwells deep within your soul. The Spirit of God is the incorruptible part of your soul. We also call it the *core of Being* of the soul.

God can directly guide only that person who turns to him in time. What does it mean to turn to God?

When you notice that you are beginning to get upset, that rage is welling up, that you want to grumble, scold, quarrel and even lash out, then turn to God in time: Talk to Him! Tell Him that you feel anger rising in you, or also tell Him that you can hardly control yourself because of your anger.

Speak to Him, and then imagine that warmth and love are radiating from inside you. Let these rays also work in you. Think: "God envelops me. God will clear up what I wanted to get upset about."

Let these warming rays go on working in you. Imagine the sun. You are lying in the sun. The sun is warming you. Its radiance calms you. It illuminates the darkness and everything is bright. You are calm and quiet. The light will bring everything to light.

Trust that God will bring everything to light, and, with God, tackle the task set by the day for you. Then you can also forgive your neighbor and ask forgiveness for your unkind thoughts.

What radiates from the depth of the soul, from the incorruptible core of Being, from God, is the direct power: God. From it comes the *direct guidance* through God.

Time and again, ask God for His direct guidance. You will then be reminded in time when anger, rage, aggression, envy, fear, strife, jealousy or other negative things arise. God calls you into your inner being in time to help you and to be able to guide you better and better, that is, more directly. Then you purify your soul much more quickly, and God radiates ever more strongly through the pure areas of your soul that are expanding.

There is also the *indirect guidance* of God. It is the guidance by means of the law of sowing and reaping. This says that whatever a person sows, he will reap, unless he clears up in time what he has caused. What a person has negatively sown and whatever part of it is active has an effect on his body.

Indirect guidance means that God radiates into your soul. However, He cannot irradiate you directly; instead, He irradiates your burdens, your causes, either so that you clear them up, or so that they can be cleared up through blows of fate and illness, so that God is then able to irradiate you directly again.

You have learned that you need not bear the effects of your causes as illnesses or blows of fate, if you listen to your conscience in time. It admonishes you and gives you hints, *before* irritation, anger, rage, hatred, envy and the like come up, if you seek out God in you and talk to Him, if you imagine Him as the sun of love and warmth, which warms you and takes everything that is dark from you.

When God can guide you directly, then He radiates through the four predominantly cleansed and now refined and light-filled soul garments or through the three fine memory garments – if you have already discarded the first four soul garments and stand in the light of fulfillment.

The three fine memory garments are the powers of preparation for the absolute life in God. These light-filled garments have the vibration of the three planes of preparation, of the three planes of light before the gate to heaven. As I already revealed to you, there, you learn to apply the Absolute Law until you are absolute again. This is already possible for you as a human being, if you turn to God in time and let yourself be enveloped, permeated and guided by His radiation of love and warmth.

If you entrust yourself to God again and again and have confidence in Him in every situation, then, via the three fine planes of light, He radiates into your world of thoughts and prepares you more and more for the absolute life in Him.

The soul garments are, so to speak, the rungs on the ladder to the divine life. These rungs are also called levels of consciousness. Once you have passed the first four levels of consciousness on the ladder to eternal life, that is, when the four dark soul garments are purified or even dissolved because they no longer have any shadows – since you have aligned your life, that is your thinking, speaking and acting, with God – you will attain the direct guidance through God more and more. You will then live in the fine radiation of Patience, Love and Mercy, in the powers of preparation before the gate to heaven, before the eternal Being, and you will then be under the direct guidance of God.

These three fine soul garments hold as a *memory* all the correspondences you have dismantled in the four purification planes. Once you live in the fine radiation of the three soul garments of Patience, Love and Mercy, that is, in the powers of preparation for the pure life in God, you will no longer have any correspondences. Your sinfulness has been overcome. But *how* you have overcome it remains as a memory in these three fine garments.

Now, when one of your brothers or sisters needs help or good advice in order to shape his or her life in a more positive manner – and if you have already overcome the same or similar aspects – then the corresponding memories become active in the three fine garments of your soul; they begin to vibrate and flow into your thoughts. Suddenly you know how you can help your neighbor in a selfless way or what you should tell him, so that through the good, selfless advice, he can find the right course for his life again. You remember how you tackled your correspondences, your soul burdens, how often you succumbed to your ego and how much or how little you had to fight until you became free of it. And so, from now on, you can selflessly serve God and your neighbor with your memories of what you once caused and have already overcome. The one who has conquered himself through the power of Christ, that is, who lives in this fine radiation of memory and thus receives and gives from the divine law, has become the true vessel of God's love and is selfless.

You must know, dear brother, dear sister, that the memories of what you have overcome must remain. With their help, you cannot only understand your fellowman who is still in the same or a similar situation as you once were – you can also serve and help him selflessly.

With the help of your memories, God, our heavenly Father, and your guardian spirit can very quickly admonish you, too, not to do the same or similar things again as you once caused. In your inner being suddenly awakens the thought: "Stop, not like this! Don't fall back into what you have already discarded. It's in you merely as a memory!"

Know that God, our heavenly Father, in Christ, your Redeemer, strives to help other human children by way of your memories. He can lead people to you, who are burdened by worries, problems, miseries and illnesses, or He leads you to them, if you have already overcome the same or similar thing. For then, you can speak from your own experience and be of help.

I repeat: God stimulates in you memories that lie in one of the three garments of preparation. You then remember how you overcame and mastered the problem or illness. And you sense how you can help your neighbor or what to say to him so he can find his way out of the situation that he is in at the moment; for you remember that once you, too, were in the same or similar situation – and how you mastered it. Suddenly you find the right words or you know, which help you may give your neighbor according to the law of life. And so, in the situation, you will know the right word, and when everything seems lost, you will know a way out.

Realize then, that this was the help of God through you for your neighbor. How wonderful it is to be guided by God so directly! Yet it requires that you have already lived through and mastered the same or similar situation yourself with the help of God or with the help of a spiritual person.

The more human aspects you have overcome with the help of the Lord, the richer you are in spiritual experiences. When it is said that God has no other hands in this world than yours, this should express that God can work through you, if you are pure for the most part.

The memories in your fine soul garments, in this fine, light-filled, lawful radiation, are thus transformers of the divine power. Via what you have overcome and which is still in you as a memory, God works in this world to stand by His human children and help them. For you, this is the direct guidance, and for your neighbor, whom God addresses through you and to whom He sends His help through you, this is the indirect guidance.

How does this take place? When a person has difficulties and is in need, and you, however, have already overcome something similar, then God leads this person to you, or He will cause you to go to the other person, if this is good for him. His difficulties emanate from him as vibrations and meet with your memories. Your memories reverberate in your consciousness and come alive in your thoughts. These let you know how you can help your neighbor or what to tell him, so that he can find his way out of his present situation.

So, the memory field in your soul begins to vibrate more intensively. The spiritual atoms of your soul that are aligned with the primordial power, with the divine core of being, then attract from the eternal, all-encompassing law the lawful answer for the person concerned. Or, the eternal law, God, shows you an inner picture of how you can help or what the person concerned would have to do, so that help can be given to him. This is the help of God through you – and for you, the direct guidance.

A lot of divine energy flows into a predominantly purified soul. As a result of the increased influx of divine power, the divine, irradiated person sees his neighbor as he is – not as he presents himself. He senses what his neighbor does not express and recognizes what he may want to conceal with his words.

When your soul is filled with light for the most part, you will look into your neighbor's gestures and facial expressions and read from his facial expression, his physical shape, his posture and also his clothing, who he is. Your neighbor need not speak – you see him.

Spiritual people, who have largely overcome the four purification planes and live in the fine radiation, know the body language of their fellowman. Nothing remains concealed to the pure one. He is in God – and God works through him and reveals all things to him. People who are solely in this fine radiation, that is, in the law of love – which means they move in pure sensations, thoughts, words and actions – have themselves become divine consciousness.

The person who lives in the fine radiation of the divine no longer needs to listen for what God speaks to him. He has become divine for the most part. And the one who has become mostly divine need no longer ask: He knows. He need no longer look: He sees. He need no longer listen for something: He hears. Recognize the fine nuances from the human to the divine!

When soul and person gradually attain the fine radiation, the three fine soul garments, then God speaks to the person more and more clearly. However, what God tells His child is not meant for second or third parties, but for this child alone!

If the person still has to listen for the word spoken to him by God, then the soul is not yet one with God. It is, however, on the way to the clear divine wellspring and to the source of the wellspring. And so, God speaks to the person through his still shadowed soul garments, in order to tell him what he should actualize within himself. But then, the burdens of his soul may no longer be severe ones! Otherwise, the fog surrounding the light of God would be too thick, for each burden is a shadow before the light of God. If the shadows before the light are still very dense, the person can receive the word of God as light and power only to a limited extent. He then hears and perceives only his *own* noises, his human ego, and mixes them with the fine impulses of God. If he wants to listen for something for himself and wants to share with his neighbor what he has heard, then he mixes the fine, indirect impulses with the noises of his human ego.

What he receives while listening for God is the *indirect guidance,* in which the impulses still come through the shadowed soul garments. This guidance is possible *only if* the person endeavors day after day to *discard* what he has recognized in himself as still needing to be cleared up: either by surrendering it to Christ or by making amends with the power of Christ and by forgiving and asking for forgiveness. *

The *direct* guidance begins when your soul lives in the fine radiation, in the three planes of preparation for heaven, which are also called filiation planes: Patience, Love and Mercy.

But the one who is still deeply rooted in the law of sowing and reaping, which applies to the four purification planes, still bears many correspondences in himself, that is, severe burdens of various degrees. God can guide such a person solely via his burdens, via the law of sowing and reaping. This means that he has to clear up, discard and no longer do

---

* To listen for God's word is in His will only when the person striving toward God is on the third level, the level of Wisdom, having actualized Order and Will for the most part, thus being active for Christ and with Christ. This means that he fulfills the law "pray and work." The daily actualization of what is recognized is decisive! It is only then that listening for the Inner Helper and Adviser is according to the law of God.

what he has recognized. This, too – as already mentioned – you can call indirect guidance.

God, the eternal light, speaks to mankind through countless mouths. By means of the energy of the day, God tells you what you should clear up today. God also speaks to the burdened soul and to the person through the incidents of the day. Each day He grants the person that amount of self-knowledge that he can deal with. God speaks to the soul and to the person through occurrences and, for example, also through people, who are still under the law of sowing and reaping. He lets us recognize ourselves in their words and in our own statements.

All of this still is the *indirect guidance* of God. By means of events, things, people, through blows of fate and illnesses, God addresses soul and person indirectly.

Everything that befalls you in the way of problems, miseries, worries, illnesses and blows of fate, does *not* come from God. You have caused it *yourself*; it is your own wrong doing toward God, the law of love and of life.

God, our heavenly Father, and your guardian spirit, as well, admonish all people in time – and you, too – before an illness breaks out or a blow of fate hits them. So, before the effect of a cause created by a person breaks out, the Spirit of God and the guardian spirit stimulate his thoughts and feelings. If the person does not listen to the voice of his conscience, or to the admonishers from without, if he continues to sin in his feelings, thoughts, words and actions, then his self-made causes flow out – the person must bear them as effects.

But God and the guardian spirit also speak to the person in the effects, that is, they speak into his conscience, as for instance: "Change your way of thinking; forgive and ask for forgiveness. Then the shadows that are effective in your body will be transformed in your soul, and the spiritual atoms will align with the primordial power, so that your soul and body are able to receive My helping and healing light."

You realize that God is active! Your guardian spirit is also very close to you and speaks into your conscience. It, too, is an admonisher, allowing certain things to happen from without, so that you awaken in your inner being.

Dear brothers and sisters, nothing could exist without the positive power, not even the negative. Thus, in everything negative there is also the positive. This means: In every defeat, in illness and misery, there is also the positive power, God.

When we address it, in illness as well as in misery and blows of fate, not by complaining, but by relying on God and profoundly praying to God, then the positive power in the negative – in illness, misery and fate – becomes active and transforms the negative, that is, the illness, misery and fate, into the positive, into health, happiness, joy and fellowship. The positive power in everything strengthens, helps and heals.

However, this requires that in all human situations you turn to God by repenting of your faults, by forgiving, asking for forgiveness and striving to no longer commit the faults you have recognized. In doing so, you are turning to God, our Father.

And so, when you surrender to God, completely trusting and believing in Him – by making amends, by forgiving and asking for forgiveness – then the spiritual atoms in the particles of your soul turn to the primordial power, to the incorruptible core of being. Through this, increased life force and light energy will then flow to you, and you will receive much light, help and healing from God – if it is for the well-being of your soul. "If it is for the well-being of your soul," means that God knows you and He knows whether you will keep your word to Him. Depending on your future behavior, God will give you what is good for your further life on earth.

If you remain in God's love and if you no longer make the old mistakes, you can be sure that what you have asked God for is already fulfilled in your soul. So your requests have already been answered. God is already active in your soul; He dissolves the shadows and radiates increased light to you – provided, as previously explained, that you keep your promise to henceforth endeavor not to make the recognized mistakes – what is against God – again. Just simply the effort is rewarded by God, our heavenly Father. This is His grace for His child.

You now realize what direct and indirect guidance is.

The day, your friend: the energy of the day – The soul travels at night – Wasted days – The beginning of the day – The journal – To listen and to hear, to see and to behold

The path to God can be compared to a ladder. Perhaps you have already heard of Jacob's ladder which, with its many rungs, reaches far into heaven. How can you check yourself to see on which rung or spiritual level you are?

Accept each day as your good friend! Know that the light of the day is energy. Each frequency of the energy of the day has its color vibration and its sound.

The day brings with itself countless frequencies, that is, color vibrations and sounds. If you have in your soul some or several of the same or like frequencies, that is, color vibrations and sounds, which radiate from your inner being, then the forces begin to flow. We call this flowing of the forces *communication.*

When communication is being established, the frequencies vibrate into your consciousness, that is, into your brain cells. They arrive there as feelings and thoughts. It is the day, your good friend, which is speaking to you. It is telling you which human aspects you should clear up this very day. It also tells you how to master a situation. For example, it shows you the beautiful things of the day, so that you can delight in them. Or it admonishes you to be kind to your parents and to all people. It may also let you stumble or even fall so that the merry-go-round of your thoughts is interrupted and you can think about the thoughts you had and whether they would please God, our heavenly Father.

There is no end to what your good friend, the day, shows you. And you can learn from everything and recognize yourself in everything. Through the energy of the day, God shows you a part of your light-filled side. Surely, you are happy about this. However, He also shows you a part of your shadowed side that you should overcome today.

The day, your good friend, brings you the strength to overcome your human aspects, to surrender them to Christ, to ask your neighbor for forgiveness and to forgive him.

Much of what you have caused may have happened years ago and has not yet been cleared up. So, if anything still needs to be taken care of – so that you can recognize yourself in it and then no longer do it – your good friend, the day, brings it to you, and you may clear it up this very day.

If you have cleared up your past for the most part, then such former incidents will remain in you as mere memories. For example, you will recall people who wronged you years ago. If you now have feelings of peace, sympathy and love for them, if you can approach them without any sense of reservation, then what had happened is forgiven. The negative has been transformed into positive power. You will recognize this by your feelings of peace, that is, by reactions such as good will and love. The former correspondences have turned into memories.

By the many incidents that the day brings you, you recognize which rung of Jacob's ladder, that is, which spiritual level, you are on.

On your way to school or at your place of work you see and hear many things. Then examine your sensations and your body's reactions! What happens in and on you? Is it composure or annoyance? From this, you recognize where you are in your spiritual development and you realize where you should ask God for help and support for your neighbor. Pray for your neighbor in every situation! Whether you have mastered the same or like things, or whether correspondences are still flaring up in you and you become irritated by your neighbor: Pray!

If you are beset by desires again and again, then something has not yet been overcome. But, if the desires just barely come up – and you tell yourself: "One day they'll be fulfilled, if it's God's will" – then they no longer pressure you, since you have matured spiritually.

All of this has something to tell you. The day leads it to you, so that you realize what you still have to clear up or what you have already cleared up – and so that you can see on which rung you stand that leads to the divine consciousness. And so, via the energy of the day, via your good friend, the day, God tells you what you should overcome today and what you have already overcome.

Dear sister, dear brother, recognize that life in the earthly garment is new each day. For each morning, shortly before you awaken, your soul returns from a journey and goes back into its earthly garment.

If you wake up during the night, then you think that your soul stayed with your body while you slept. Or in the morning, when you awaken, you think that your soul was always with your body and in it, because you open your eyes and perceive the same surroundings again as the day before. And yet, it is different.

Although your good friend has remained the same on the new day, it brings along events and impressions for you quite different from those of the previous day. For today you do not feel or think as you did the day before.

So, today, the new day, has in store yet other frequencies and sounds for you. The same or like vibrating aspects lie in you. Again the day stimulates these soul vibrations – and already the new program for the day begins for you: The day's frequencies that are meant for you stimulate the program of your soul, that is, various vibrations in your soul, through which communication results. It, in turn, vibrates into your brain cells, into your world of thoughts, and you are then able to perceive what God and your guardian spirit want to tell you via your good friend, the day.

And so, they can tell you that it would be good to clear up this or that. You sense it in your conscience and perceive it in your thoughts. You do it and you feel: "You did well, that was selfless. Be happy about it!"

The good friend also helps you with your schoolwork. When you are clear in your mind and have no confused, that is insignificant, thoughts, then you can perceive the countless aids that the day brings you. It is God, your heavenly Father, and your guardian spirit who are active via your good friend, the day.

In which realms of the beyond your soul was while your body lay in deep sleep is essential for the energy of the day, for the course of each day,.

At night, when your body is fast asleep, your soul goes on a journey. However, it is connected to your body by the so-called silver cord or information cord. This maintains the link between your soul body and your sleeping physical body while the soul is outside of your body.

Take note that your human body can fall asleep only when your soul, which is filled with energy and provides your body with energy, slowly withdraws from your body. According to its gradual withdrawal, you then fall asleep. The energies diminish, and therefore, your body sleeps. Once you are deeply asleep, your soul can leave your body entirely. But it remains connected to it. If, however, your sleep is only light, it is impossible for your soul to step entirely out of your body.

It all depends on how you behaved during the day. If you were very nervous during the day and can therefore not attain a deep sleep, then the soul is unable to leave your body entirely. If, however, you lived your day consciously and in harmony, if the day's work was successful for you because your good friend, the day, was able to help you, then you will go to sleep calmly, and the soul can completely withdraw from your body while it lies in deep slumber. And so, the more deeply you sleep the further away the soul can go from its body.

I repeat: If you have over-exerted yourself physically during the day or were preoccupied with many unimportant things and thoughts, then you are nervous and your sleep is light, since not only your consciousness but also your subconscious is burdened with events and things that have not been dealt with. This means that your soul leaves your body only partially, that is, it does not reach other worlds – because you did not sleep deeply enough.

Surely, you have experienced that while falling asleep you suddenly jerk. It is a strong twitch of your body, and suddenly you are wide awake again. This is the moment in which your soul quickly re-enters your body. These jerky movements show you that your soul was indeed partially outside your body, but had not yet gone away from you. Shortly before you woke up completely, it rapidly slipped back into your body. This sudden movement of your body occurs only when you are not fast asleep – when dropping off, for example, or during a very light sleep.

But it may also be the case that when no further disturbance occurs, you might also notice this jerking while falling asleep – but you continue to calmly sleep on. At that point, you noticed that your soul left your body. Your soul felt that you would continue to sleep and it could therefore go on its journey.

Disturbances may not come solely from the outside, but also through your subconscious. When the soul begins to disengage itself from the body – namely, when you fall asleep – something can briefly move in your subconscious. If occurrences are touched in this process that rise in your consciousness, then this fetches you back from falling asleep. The soul then quickly slips back into its body. But your soul always remains connected with your body through the information cord – no matter where it is.

When you wake up after a longer sound sleep, it is very rare that you will experience these jerky movements, because the body has communicated its gradual awakening in time to the journeying soul through the silver cord, and your soul is already in your body when you open your eyes. You then wake up calmly without knowing where your soul has been.

You may say: "It would be interesting to see where the soul stays at night, what it does, which impressions it brings back with it." Well, these need not remain concealed from you – if you cleanse your soul from the shadows of your wrongdoing and keep your consciousness and your subconscious largely free of major burdens, of human thoughts and physical excitation. And so, when you are relaxed and largely free from pressing desires, from worries and problems and from human thoughts concerning your neighbor, then your soul can reflect its impressions into your person: Your free consciousness and subconscious then absorb the impressions of your soul, which it has brought from the other worlds, in the pictorial language of the soul. Then, you experience what has been reflected into your soul as a dream that is true or even when you are awake right after awaking. You then know that it is so. For often the dream that is true includes recognition for yourself.

We also call dreams that are true, waking dreams or lucid dreams. Among other things, they show you on which rung of the ladder to the consciousness of God the soul stands or what the soul is presently working on, which is still hidden to the person.

The reflections in the soul are symbols, that is, pictures, because the language of the soul is a language of pictures – it is the language of consciousness. This is why you can discern in the symbolism of a dream that is true on which level of consciousness you are. The soul also reflects into you its inner liberation or its still existing ties to outer things and people.

It is worthwhile to observe and fulfill the laws of God and to accept the day gratefully. Its energy is the inspirer, which lets you realize what you have to clear up in your life on earth today. The energy of the day is also the transformer for the admonishments from the divine and from the guardian spirit.

And so, the day is your good friend. No matter what it brings you – be it your memories so that you can lawfully help your neighbor, or your correspondences, so that you settle today what needs to be cleared up – Christ, your Redeemer, stands by you!

Life gives a person many experiences and enriches his inner being, if he takes in the impulses of the day and lives according to them.

Dear sister, dear brother, many are already walking the path to God. Do you want to take part? Then participate:

Accept these explanations and try them out first – for the one who has gained his very own experiences will walk the Inner Path joyfully. Many people can accept the gifts of God from the law of love only when they have gained their own experiences. God, our heavenly Father, also helps those who first require their own experiences in order to then walk the path to Him more consciously and more oriented toward the goal.

Try it out on yourself and learn through your personal experience what I will explain to you now. – First let me describe the course of a day as many people experience it:

Many do not take control of their own thinking and acting and thereby waste their days. They let the days come and go – without paying attention to what the days have brought to them, what they wanted and want to tell them. They take the days for granted. They wake up, get out of bed and think, think, think – uncontrolled.

While washing his body and getting dressed, the person thinks, thinks and thinks about all kinds of things, whatever comes to his mind. He turns essential and nonessential thoughts over in his mind. This is how he already slips into a merry-go-round of thoughts in the morning. All sorts of thoughts turn and move, and often, he is not even aware of this. He lets himself be controlled by all sorts of thoughts and desires.

At breakfast, he then talks and talks to his family or to those who sit at the table with him. He does not notice that his neighbor may have a day's rhythm that is totally different from his own. He always wants to see himself in the center of the stage and speaks out whatever comes to mind or is on the tip of his tongue. He is annoyed or glad, depending on what he thought or whom he thought of.

The subconscious and conscious mind of someone who spends his life like this is filled with uncontrolled thinking and speaking.

On the way to school or to work the merry-go-round of thoughts goes on and on. When he meets school friends or colleagues at work, he talks, talks and talks – without giving a thought to whether what he says is important or unimportant, whether it is of interest for his neighbor or not. He talks only from his own ego.

The conscious mind and the subconscious of someone who behaves this way are stuffed with all sorts of things, thoughts or desires – and are clogged up against good and lawful inputs, against the impulses from the day. Only his ego flows out from him. That is why he can hardly be guided by the divine impulses and his guardian spirit, and little of his quota for the day, which he should put into practice today, enter his awareness. He talks only from what he himself has input, from his ego.

The result is that in school or at his place of work he continues to think about what moves in his conscious mind and in his subconscious. Therefore, he cannot grasp and put into practice his quota of work at school or at work to the extent he should, for his consciousness, his subconscious and his soul garments are filled with his own thought patterns, desires and ideas.

Already during the morning, he no longer sees the sun for all his egocentric clouds. This means that he does not receive what the day wants to tell him. He thinks about the past; he thinks about the future; he thinks about his problems and the trouble with his or her life partner, with his children or grand-parents, his schoolmates or colleagues at work. On the side, he more or less does his work, which, in the end, does not interest him greatly, because he constantly has to think about himself and about the things that this or that person has done or might do to him.

Lunch then goes like breakfast: He thinks and thinks; he talks and talks. It is similar in the evening: He thinks, thinks, talks, talks – and finally, a television program diverts his thoughts.

What has such a person experienced? Only himself! But, more often than not, he is probably not even aware of this. What has he recognized and cleared up? Little or nothing. Thus, he has not made use of the day. So we can say that the past as well as his desires and ideas have lived him, so to speak. He let his correspondences live through him – and, at the same time, he reinforced them, since he thought and talked only about *his* own affairs. Thoughts and words are forces. With them, he has continued to build up and thereby intensify his human programs and burdens. This is why, he has not fulfilled his work quota to the degree he could have if he had curbed his thoughts and concentrated on his work instead of turning his problems over in his mind.

And so, he recognized little or nothing compared to a person who is alert for the impulses of the day and who settles what needs to be cleared up. Neither the teacher nor the employer is satisfied with such a person – no matter what occupation he has, whether he is a student, employee, worker, doctor, engineer or artisan. Such people, who because of their limited consciousness think only about themselves, are, at school or business or wherever they are, quite often the black sheep who talk a lot, yet, accomplish little.

Dear brother, dear sister, in the evening, examine whether your day has passed in a similar fashion as described. Your feelings and your conscience tell you this!

Every day is interesting if a person takes an interest in it, if he makes use of it, pays attention to it, accepts it as a good friend early in the morning and thanks God that the new day has come to him again.

Every person waking up in the morning is at first approached by the day, resembling a veiled figure. Under its veil, it bears what the person should take care of and clear up today, whether in his private life, at school or at work. The friend also helps to fulfill the day's task quota and provides good, even very good, impulses to think about.

You know by now that nothing happens by chance. Everything is predetermined and controlled by the energy that works directly or indirectly – through your seed, which is energy as well, or through the direct energy of God. The direct energy of God *guides* soul and person, the indirect energy, your seed, *controls* them.

Every person is either *controlled* indirectly by the law of sowing and reaping, namely, by the programs he himself has entered into his soul – or he is *guided* directly by God, the inner life, without the interposition of the law of sowing and reaping.

You have already read and absorbed the fact that direct guidance is possible only once you have left the law of sowing and reaping and your soul is able to absorb the light-filled energy of God. The indirect guidance, or control, takes place via the seed, via the causes created by yourself, which are in your soul as programs.

Be alert for the day's impulses! Experience and learn about yourself in them – and you will recognize yourself.

Dear sister, dear brother, purchase a notebook which you can use as a *journal*. It should be handy enough that you can carry it with you, the boy in his suit, the girl in her handbag, or in a schoolbag or briefcase. Where you keep it is quite up to you. The journal becomes interesting when you make your entries conscientiously!

It is possible that your parents kept a *book of insights* for you up to your twelfth year of age. If there is one like that and you wish to continue it as a journal, you can do so; it is completely up to you.

Ask your parents to complete the book of insights, and, if you wish, to write a dedication to you with their perceptions of you, their child. This would certainly be a nice conclusion to your childhood days and, at the same time, it could be the foundation for you on which you can build and from which you can see what is still waiting to be cleared up, which strengths, but also weaknesses you had in your childhood and possibly still have.

You begin with your journal now. In the morning the day's first experience takes place: Your soul carried out a small reincarnation; it came back into its body again from another world. So, you are awake again. Did you have a dream? Do you still know your dream? Does it seem to be important? If it does, make a few notes in your journal!

The first thing to do after waking up should be to give thanks to God for the new day. Ask God, your heavenly Father, and your Redeemer, Christ, to enable you to accept the day as it comes to you and however it presents itself. In your prayer also think of the people whom you know you will meet today. They are your parents, your brothers or sisters, or your grandparents. If you still go to school, they are your teachers and fellow students. If you are already employed, send good thoughts to your colleagues and to the ones in charge or the "boss."

Send good thoughts as well to all those whom you will meet on the street and whom you might wonder about. Nothing happens by chance! Know that when a passer-by attracts your attention, this wants to tell you something. Either you should pay attention to your correspondences or you should send the passer-by caring thoughts. Through this, something in your soul as well as in your neighbor's soul can be dissolved that has perhaps still tied you to each other. Your thoughts tell you whether you are still not clear with your neighbor. Or you know his soul from the soul realms – or your soul remembers the spirit being which is now in the human being, and which perhaps was and is very closely linked with you in heaven.

In this way, you accept the still veiled day.

In the course of your earthly and spiritual development, every day will become a good friend of yours. For not only does it bring you *knowledge* about your humanness, but it also tells you how you should tackle it in order to overcome it. Learn to listen to your friend, and it will serve you as advisor and not only as a herald.

When you don't only listen to what your neighbors are saying, when you don't only see what comes into your range of vision – when, therefore, you don't only register the externalities – but instead become accustomed to *hearing* what your friend, the day, wants to tell you through people, things, occurrences and events; and when you not only see what is obvious but learn to *behold* – that is, when you let the things you have heard and seen first work in you by *correctly listening* and *correctly looking*, too – then you will hear what your friend, the day, says to you, and you will behold what your friend conveys to you about what your neighbor does not speak out.

Know that most people merely hear the words and do not listen to what is behind the word or inside the word. Most people look only at the person and do not behold the way he really is. And so, you recognize the subtle difference between listening and hearing, between seeing and beholding.

The *one who hears* is a curious person or a person who wants to grasp everything with his intellect. He hears only what is said and does not listen to what is unspoken. He cannot listen to what is behind the words or listen into the words and discern what remains unspoken.

The one who merely *sees* recognizes and grasps only what his own soul garments, his correspondences and the content of his consciousness and subconscious convey to him. Therefore, he sees only the appearance, that is, what seems to be obvious, but is not reality. He looks past reality.

The person who *beholds* lets the situation and the matter first have an effect on him. For this reason, he does not react spontaneously, but lets everything first approach him, in order to view the whole correctly. This means that he first of all takes the present situation and matter into himself. From this, a communication arises between these impressions and the divine in him.

This communication then activates the spiritual forces in the person's soul. They vibrate into his conscious mind, and the one turned to God beholds what others do not see; he hears what others do not hear – and thereby he knows how to master the situation and matter.

This means to not think and speak about a situation and matter the very moment you hear and see it, but let it first have its effect in you.

God, the Life, thus tells you via your good friend, the day, how you should react in the various situations and matters, how you should tackle or overcome them, thus making proper use of the moments of the day.

The very moment you wake up in the morning, that is, when you open your eyes, your good friend, the day, approaches you with the first thoughts. It already brings some essential thoughts that are decisive for your day. You recognize them by the fact that they please you and that you immediately know what is to be done. Note these thoughts in your journal at once.

The insignificant thoughts – we also call them vagabond thoughts – which come flying at you now and then, intending to influence and cloud you, that is, muddle you, give over at once to Christ, your Redeemer. Immediately pray fervently and thank Him with all your heart for the past night, for the new day and for your health. If during the morning toilette further important thoughts should come to you, note these down in your journal, too.

Afterward, if possible before breakfast, sit down quietly and upright on a chair and pray to God with all your heart. Thank Him for your life on earth. Thank Him for your waking up in the morning. Thank Him again for the new day, which you have gratefully accepted from God's hand. Thank Him for the new strength and for the secureness within your family. Thank Him for your parents who care about you, who took care of you as a child and who still care for you now. In your prayer also think about all the people on earth; think about the misery and illness, the light and darkness.

After your prayer or after breakfast – whenever you have a bit of time – reflect on the thoughts that you wrote down. Listen into the words, into whatever you have noted down, and sense what your good friend, the day, wanted to tell you with them. The day wants to tell you how you can absorb and actualize the things you wrote down.

For instance, thoughts concerning school or thoughts about your work already contain the answer. Your friend, the day, helps you listen and see into the answer, so that you may know what is going on in you, what needs to be done and how you can deal with this.

Every hint contains the solution; it is just waiting to be taken in and *actualized.* In every question, there lies a lawful answer, because in everything there is the power, the love and wisdom of God. Therefore each question and every answer contains the solution at the same time, as well.

Recognize: The unlawful also contains the solution, the positive. In every problem, in every difficulty, in all that happens is the Spirit of God, His help – and thus the solution. Is this not wonderful?

I repeat: The solution, the positive, the good is in all things. It is the Spirit of God, our heavenly Father, who knows about all things, who knows you, because you are His child.

Correlations between soul, fine-material stars and planets and material stars and planets – The influence of energy fields in the earth's atmosphere and of earth-bound souls – Turn to Christ, your Redeemer!

God, our heavenly Father, wants to stand by you and help you, so that you not go astray and are not led astray.

God, your heavenly Father, and your guardian spirit endeavor in many ways to protect you from your own wrong doing and also from being led astray by your fellowman who, for example, may even encourage you to do things that are unlawful, that is, sinful.

The one who acts against the divine law or tempts his fellowman to do so burdens his soul. And even those who were servile, who carried out what you perhaps had forced on them, burden themselves. Therefore, be on your guard!

The instigator – in this case, you – burdens himself more. The perpetrators burden themselves as well, according to their spiritual knowledge, their spiritual responsibility and their actions. Because of their violations of the divine law, that is, because of their burden, you – as the instigator – and the perpetrators are tied together by the causal cord. The causal cord is an invisible cord that ties those people together in the law of sowing and reaping who have created causes together.

Therefore, pay attention to your behavior and never force your will upon your neighbor – that he should do what you think is right! Bear in mind that every word and every action that is unlawful, that is, not in accordance with the divine law, can become your downfall. Often, you will not experience the effect immediately.

The repository, your soul, registers your lawful, selfless, divine behavior as well as your unlawful, godless, human behavior. What is stored by the soul, the positive as well as the negative, is also registered by the fine-material stars, the purification planets. You have heard that in the Spirit similarly vibrating things attract each other. According to their vibration, the fine-material stars take in those souls that have discarded their physical body, and serve temporarily as their dwelling place.

You also have already read that a person is guided indirectly by God for as long as he lives in the law of sowing and reaping.

The law of the eternal Father is love. The love radiation, the eternal law, maintains all souls and people – as well as all heavenly bodies in the whole of infinity. God's law of love also radiates into those stars that have stored your positive and your negative qualities. When one of God's rays touches one of your causes that are registered in a planet, then the cause in your soul is activated at the same time. However, before it breaks out, God, your heavenly Father, and your guardian spirit admonish you – via the events of the day.

I repeat: When God, our Lord, leads you indirectly, that is, via the day, through people's words, gestures and actions or through so-called coincidental occurrences, then God, the Absolute Law, the law of love, initiates this via the stars.

All people and all souls still living in the law of sowing and reaping are under the influence of the material stars and are more or less led by them – depending on their soul burdens.

You know the signs of the zodiac and you have certainly heard about the constellations of the stars. The constellations of the material stars are transformers of the energies that come from the fine-material planets, that is, from the soul realms, in which your causes are stored – as they are stored in your soul.

Now you can understand that each soul, including those incarnated in a human body, is linked via a so-called radiation or information cord with those purification planets in which its causes are stored. The light of a soul reaches only as far as its consciousness is developed and according to this, souls and people are guided.

Many burdened souls and people are in close communication with energy fields in the earth's atmosphere. They call up information from there. These energy fields can also be brought into movement by the fine-material purification planets in which the causes are stored that were created under the law of sowing and reaping.

The one who does not align his life with God, but with extraterrestrial powers, also attracts souls from the beyond, which then, through him, carry out their own interests – which ultimately are also present in him as correspondences. Souls whose interests vibrate according to the pertinent energy fields can also influence him.

When a person's soul is under the influence of these forces, then the person, too, is a captive of the earth because his soul is not oriented toward heaven, but is satisfied with the radiations from such spheres. The soul of a person who is very attached to the world is likewise tied to the earth, if he is concerned only about his material well-being.

When a soul that is tied to the earth leaves its dying body, it cannot enter the light of God. It will continue to remain tied to the earth until it awakens in Christ and is resurrected through Christ.

There are many such souls on earth; they are invisible to the human eye. These souls are able to influence people who are captives of the earth, that is, people whose every thought and desire are oriented to matter, who focus only on what they can see, hear, smell, taste and touch. These are people who nurture their base, human ego and who influence their fellowman – that is, they have a determinant effect on them – and demand things of them that are unlawful.

They strive only to possess, to be and to have. Thus, these people can be influenced by negative energy fields or by souls tied to the earth. Heavy smokers, drinkers, gluttons – to say, sybaritic, pleasure-seeking people – as well as drug addicts or people who are strongly sexually inclined can also be influenced by atmospheric energy fields or by earth-bound souls.

It is only selfless love, the love for God and neighbor, that can lead you away from such dangers and protect you from such influences. Therefore, the highest commandment for you, and ultimately for every person, should be to develop selfless love – the law of God that leads to inner freedom and independence.

Through His sacrifice on Golgotha, Christ, the Son of God, your Redeemer, took on every soul and every human being. With His "It is finished," He detached a part of the primordial energy, His divine inheritance, from the Primordial Central Sun, divided it and transferred a spark of it to each soul. Through this, every soul has become stabilized. This means that it cannot regress in its development to such a level that it would have to perhaps incarnate in an animal body or even turn into the radiation of plants or stones.

Some religions teach that souls can incarnate in animals, plants or stones. This is not in accordance with the universal law of God – the darkness wanted it. However, Christ prevented it through His Redeemer-deed.

You know from the book "I Give Advice – Do You Accept?" that stones, plants and animals are the life from God. They are still in the evolutionary process toward a perfect spirit body, which will be raised to the filiation of God. Stones, plants and the lower species of animals have no soul. They are in a so-called collective. This means that as equally developed species they are irradiated and vivified by the light of God and also further developed by the eternal law.

Since through the sacrifice on Golgotha, every soul has received the power that provides it with stability and maintains the filiation from the divine inheritance of the Redeemer, Christ, it can never fall so far that it will regress in its development via the animals, plants and stones and finally be just a ray that once again has to resume its path of evolution, from stone via plant, animal and nature being to a child of God.

For your understanding I repeat: A soul can incarnate neither in an animal nor in a plant or a stone. The Redeemer-power has saved it from this. Through His Redeemer-deed, Christ has accepted all souls and people.

You will surely inquire when Christ can receive you. He can receive you when you let yourself be received by Him. This means, when you turn toward your Redeemer, the light of God in you – when you strive to become selfless.

To become selfless means to want to please God, alone, by keeping peace with your fellowman, by not railing at them, but by being understanding of them, by thinking and speaking lovingly and kindly and by helping people who need help – without asking for reward or recognition. This is selflessness.

God, our heavenly Father in Christ, and your guardian spirit help you to become selfless. They guide you indirectly and show you whether you are already selfless or what you still need to work on.

As you now know, you experience the manifold, indirect guidance through the Spirit of God by way of the energy of the day – that is, via the events of the day, via people you meet, and also via your parents, grandparents, relatives, teachers, colleagues or boss at work. You experience whether you are selfless or what you still need to work on – via passersby, playing children, and all people and things that you notice and that cause you to think. Your senses of hearing, of smell, taste and touch, too, may trigger thoughts in you that tell you what you have already cleared up or have not yet cleared up, and what needs to be actualized, now.

Be alert and endeavor to clear up your human aspects by asking for forgiveness and by forgiving, when, for example, you had a strong argument or even a fight with someone. If you then don't create the same or like causes anymore, you have been received by Christ.

Through your positive, lawful life, you expand your consciousness. The Christ-light in you begins to shine more intensely and to radiate throughout you. More and more, you behold things and events in the proper light. If you then sense, think, speak and act according to your spiritual development, you will be resurrected by Christ and in Christ.

After your physical death, you will no longer be an earthbound soul. Your light-filled soul will go to the light-filled, fine-material planets that have the same vibration as you. Remember that the help is in you. It is the Spirit of the Christ of God, your Redeemer.

Nothing happens by chance: Everything is guided or controlled – Man's self-programming

As your sister from the Light, I, Liobani, may now tell you how you can sense, think, speak and act in the right way – that is, lawfully. So that you may better understand me, I will go a little deeper in my explanations:

You can compare your soul and your body to a computer. Just as the computer is programmed – that is, stores data – so does the person program his consciousness and his subconscious – his brain cells – and his soul, the particles of his soul. Thus, he programs himself with his sensations, thoughts, words and actions. This programming then controls him. This control also has an effect on his five senses: The person sees, hears, smells, tastes and touches according to his self-programming.

During the course of his life on earth, each person has stored several programs in his soul. Insofar as they are active, they are connected with the same or similar programs in the earth's atmosphere. I also call this connection *communication.*

Programs are energy complexes, also called energy fields, which are comprised of innumerable sensations, thoughts, words and activities.

An example for this: Your way to school is also based on a program, which you have set up for yourself with the help of your parents, grandparents or school friends. You have, for example, thought about which way or ways to school you should choose – and you have tried them out.

Before choosing the way or ways, you considered which way might be shorter, which one is pleasant to walk, which houses you pass by, which people live there, which people you will meet, and similar things. All this you have absorbed into yourself. This is now a program that is stored in your brain cells.

Again and again, this program – also called an energy field or energy complex – seeks communication, a connection with an energy field that corresponds to it, for example, with the one that corresponds to your way to school. You then communicate with that energy complex, and will thus very often, as if automatically, take the same way to school.

If you have, for example, tried out several ways to school, various small programs have developed in you. Now and then, you think: "Well, sometime I'll choose a different way to school." In the following days this thought crops up quite often – and all of a sudden, you do take a different way!

See, this, too, is not by chance – just as nothing in life happens by chance. In all of infinity, nothing happens by chance! Everything is held in good order by the invisible power that we call God, or also the law of God. In all of infinity, there is nothing that is outside the law of God. Everything, even the smallest speck of dust, is subject to the divine law. The law of sowing and reaping, the causal law, is also permeated by the divine, that is, by the Absolute Law, God, and is subject to it.

Whether your soul is already filled with light and energy – that is, living in the law of God – or is still in the law of sowing and reaping, you are governed by the Absolute Law, God!

Nothing happens by chance. Everything is controlled or guided.

The eternal truth radiates into this world in many facets. And so, I will explain to you, by yet another facet of the eternal truth, the expressions "controlled" and "guided":

The one who is still in the law of sowing and reaping, in the causal law, is *controlled* by his causes, the shadows of his soul. It is true that the Absolute Law is active in everything that exists, in all things, in people, souls, stars and planets, in animals, plants and stones. But as long as the person still lives in the causal law, the eternal law has only an indirect effect, by way of the law of sowing and reaping. This means that it affects the person's causes, his shadows – because the eternal law cannot completely permeate soul and person.

You can imagine this as follows: The causes of the person, the shadows of his soul, can be compared to a dam. The dam is the hindrance. It does not allow the eternal law to flow completely. And so, it rejects the stream of God. The stream of God does indeed flow as a tiny trickle through the dam – it is the life force that just barely maintains the person; one could say: that just barely keeps the physical body alive. Everything else happens through the latent or active shadows, which mark and influence the person.

The stream of God, the divine radiation, is unable to permeate matter or the soul unhindered, because the shadows, the burdens, are in its way; but the radiation touches one or several areas of the shadows. These areas of the shadows of the human ego then become activated; they control soul and person and move the things made by the person and to which he is still tied.

The energy of the day, in which the light of God is active, also sets things, souls and people into motion and brings to light the good as well as the not so good, or the bad as you call it.

All this is controlled by what you yourself have once input, that is, by your program, your causes. And so, whatever is active in your soul, what you have caused in this or an earlier life on earth – that is, what lies in your soul or in your subconscious or your consciousness – controls you.

So, in your earthly life, it depends on the burdening of your soul, but above all, on your actualization: Either you are *controlled* by your self-made law, or *guided* by God, the eternal law.

When you attentively watch your reactions, you can recognize this, for example, when you meet certain kinds of people or when you stumble, when you drop an object or when your neighbor says something you cannot agree with or even insults you. You recognize the control or guidance by the way you react, whether you become agitated, think or speak negatively and insult your neighbor as well – or whether you remain at ease and calm, regardless of who or what approaches you.

The following may also be possible: On your way to school, for instance, you meet the same people over and over again. You see them and go by without thinking about them. Perhaps you greet one or the other passer-by in a very friendly manner, because you meet him again and again, but you do not dwell on him. This can go on for days, weeks or even months. Suddenly, on this very day, you can no longer greet one of these passers-by freely. In your inner being, ill will suddenly starts to rise against this person. You notice that his attitude annoys you – although he has had this attitude all along. You just did not see it consciously before. What could lie behind this?

The soul of the passer-by and your soul are linked by causes. In one of your previous lives, you created causes. Today's energy of the day has stirred up these aspects in your soul. What does the energy of the day, your good friend, wish to tell you through this turmoil in your emotions? It wants to tell you: Ask this person's soul for forgiveness! You need not talk to this person, because he knows nothing about it, only you sense this. If you were to ask the soul of this passer-by for forgiveness for what once occurred – whereby it is not necessary for you to know *what* is at the root of it – fine rays go out from you to this person's soul. According to the soul's degree of maturity, it automatically or even consciously takes in these fine vibrations. What was present as causes in both souls, that is, in you and in your neighbor, the passer-by on the street, can be thus transformed, that is, taken away – or only a partial burden remains in you and in your neighbor's soul. It depends on the intensity of the burden.

It is also possible that everything may be cleared up in you, but not yet in the passer-by's soul, because the energy of the day could not yet reach him through the constellation of the planets. So, it can be that you will meet him again in this earthly existence and that he may go through a similar experience as you did, today.

Or the two of you will not meet each other again until another earthly life, or as souls in the spheres of purification, if at that time there are still corresponding causes in both of you.

However, if everything is erased in you and if only a remainder of causes is left in your neighbor's soul, then *you* need not encounter him again, not even in the soul realms. The soul may cross your path a couple of times in the spheres of purification, or the person here on this earth. The soul, as well as the person, may still have its difficulties with you in its thoughts – as your own experience was now. You yourself, however, must neither meet nor see him again.

Nevertheless, if you do meet him, because it is good for him, so that he can recognize himself again and again, then you, who have become free toward him, will greet him in a friendly, loving manner, which may help the soul and the person to discard what still smolders in him against you. If when meeting him again, your heart and mind stay calm, you can assume that much or even all of what was in you against him has been cleared up.

You can recognize from this example what is control and what is guidance: For as long as there is still something to be cleared up between people, they are *controlled*. At a given time they are led to each other. When in your soul everything is cleared up for the most part, then your shadows become brighter, and very gradually *guidance* begins: You will then meet many people, too, – but in you, there is peace and radiating love.

So pay attention to your behavior toward people and things! You will then recognize whether it is control or guidance that leads you.

Recognize that when you, for example, take offense at an event or a person and become annoyed about it, then this matter or encounter wants to tell you something – for nothing happens by chance.

Every irritation shows you that something in yourself is not in order, that is, a cause lies in you. Never is the thing or matter or the person the sole author of your irritation. Therefore, you should first take a look at your own self!

Let me speak about your way to school again: Now, week after week, you take the same way to school. Suddenly, it occurs to you to take a different way today. What is at the root of this – presuming that nothing happens by chance?

What happens to you on the different way today can provide you with further impulses for recognizing yourself and clearing up what you recognize as being human in you. What you have recognized should then be put into practice.

Or an acquaintance comes and takes you along in his car. If you are guided, you will experience great joy, for through the day, God has given you a gift for your selfless love and kindness, which you have given to your fellowman in this or one of your previous lives. This, then, was the direct guidance by the Absolute Law of God's love.

God, our Father, is kind.

Find the positive in everything that is unlawful – Lawful answers and solutions – Address the negative via the positive!

You have heard that in everything negative there is the positive.

The positive is the solution for everything that comes to you. The positive forces tell you how you can overcome the unlawful, the human aspects, and which steps you should take. The positive powers also tell you that the way that you are now thinking and speaking, that is, the way you are communicating, is what you still are. When something unlawful happens to you – be it only a brief welling up of envy and jealousy in you – then search in it for the positive as a solution! As you have heard, in every irritation, in every human aspect, is the seed of the positive as a help toward recognition and actualization.

Pray a lot, and ask the Christ of God, the Spirit in you, again and again, for inner guidance and for recognition in everything! With this request to the Spirit of God for His help to recognize and to clear up your human aspects, you nudge the seed, the positive power. Through this, it begins to vibrate more intensely and then seeks a way in you to reveal itself to you. At what time and in which way the solution will come to you, leave up to God, your heavenly Father in Christ, your Redeemer. Trust that you will receive the solution from God's hands at *exactly* the time that is good for you.

A person is also tied to everything that he binds to himself. When the works of the person are against the divine law, then they are permeated by the causal law, the law of sowing and reaping, and the person who has created them is tied to his human work.

When the works of the person, what he has created, are in God's will, that is, in the law of God, then what he does is blessed and permeated by the law of love.

Good people whose souls are filled with light do not bind their fellowman to themselves. For they do not expect their fellowman to do what they personally consider to be right. Light-filled people are understanding, tolerant and of good will. Their works and their deeds correspond to this. This spiritual attitude leads to selfless love and to a genuine service for their neighbor. The works of such people are good and serve the common good, not only their own good.

Selfish people think solely of themselves. Whatever they do: They want to be exalted and acknowledged.

Understanding, tolerance and good will do not imply that you should condone the negative deeds of your neighbor!

However, do not speak negatively about your neighbor and what he does, because every person is on a different level of consciousness and may not be in a position to realize what he is doing at the moment. The spiritual person may address such a person about his faults and weaknesses, but should not hold this against him.

According to the law of God, the selfless love, a spiritual person strives to address the negative via the positive. This means to find the positive in every human aspect, in all negative talking and doing, and to *first* address this positive, and only then the negative! You will find many positive aspects in your neighbor through understanding, tolerance and good will toward him. Base your conversation on these positive aspects and then carefully direct it to the faulty behavior and deeds.

The one who addresses the positive first also finds the right words for the unlawful aspects, in order to draw his neighbor's attention to them. Recognize that this way of carrying out a conversation, to approach the negative by means of the positive, is the step toward impersonal thinking, speaking and acting. You will now ask: "What is personal and what is impersonal?" I will come back to this in my explanations. Be patient.

I now come to speak again of the solution that is contained in everything negative:

For example, you meet schoolmates or teachers from your school. You notice that not everyone is looking happy. One is being sullen, the other does not return your greeting although he heard you. Yet another hangs his head because he is brooding over heavy thoughts; the next is friendly, his eyes radiate happiness.

This is how it would be right to behave: Be understanding toward all of them, for you, too, are often in the same or like situation! They are being controlled or guided according to the burdening of their souls. When, for example, you are talking with your schoolmates be aware of the fact that each question, each word, every sentence contains the solution as well, the answer that you can give according to the law of God.

When you speak or write in a positive, that is, selfless way, you do not have to search for the words, the solution; your word is then clear and unequivocal. You first sense in yourself what you should say or write. This means that before you answer, speak, write or act, you should first let what you have heard or read reverberate in you.

In every person, in you, as well, is the All-consciousness. It is the incorruptible Spirit, God, the all-permeating power, which is effective in all Being. Thus, the Spirit of God gives you the lawful answer to every question and the lawful solution to every difficulty and every problem.

You can receive lawful answers and solutions only from the All-consciousness, the omnipresent, flowing Spirit, God. For this to be possible, it requires that you no longer judge and condemn your fellowman, that you no longer judge his words and actions, but let understanding prevail. Then you will also receive from within.

However, to be understanding does not mean that you should affirm that people remain what many of them are: human and negative, which means unlawful toward almost everything.

When you accept your ego again and again, in order to recognize and overcome it by giving its facets over to Christ and, if necessary, asking your neighbor for forgiveness and forgiving him and making amends for what you have caused, then you will increasingly live in yourself and draw closer to the divine in your inner being.

The closer you draw to the divine primordial source, the more your answers are within the divine law. And the solutions to all difficulties and problems will also then come from the pure source, God, in you. It is the divine, the incorruptible in your soul, which shows you the solution to all problems and difficulties. From there, the lawful answers flow to you in all conversations and to all questions.

The answers and the solutions that the Spirit of God, the eternal law of love, gives you, are *impersonal.*

The impersonal does not value-judge. It makes itself known in a way that does not harm you and your neighbor. The impersonal leaves to each soul and to each person their free will. It does not coerce the neighbor. It merely gives advice and help, and leaves it up to you and your neighbor to take a different course of action. The impersonal in you is the divine adviser, who does not act in a determinant fashion.

A lawful, impersonal answer and solution comes from your inner being only when you strive to let go of your human aspects, in order to draw closer to the primordial stream, the All-consciousness. And so, do not judge and condemn, because everything that goes out from you comes back to you!

When speaking with your neighbor – with your parents, relatives, with schoolmates and teachers – remember my words: Stay impersonal! Find *within yourself* the right contribution to a conversation: the lawful answer and also the just solution to difficulties and problems.

How do you find your way to God in your inner being, to the inner God who is the All-consciousness, the primordial Spirit?

First of all, pull back your senses! Do not just look at outer appearances. Everything external, whatever it seems to be, bears within the good, the divine, the Being. Do not just hear the human words. Listen, into your inner being, and you will find the meaning in them.

Do not ponder about what is spoken, either. First take in what has been said. Now ask God for the right answer, for a lawful conversation. Then you will receive!

Know that the person, the base ego, disparages very quickly, thereby forming a judgment. The one who disparages wants, in turn, to exalt himself with this. The one who disparages others in order to exalt himself has little spirituality. He lacks the divine energies. To disparage means to imply something about someone or to malign his character with human aspects. Whoever does so wants to imply: "I'm better than my neighbor." That is exalting oneself.

So, take yourself back and strive to take in what your neighbor is saying! You succeed in doing so only if you have *accepted* your neighbor, that is, when you do not disparage him, but listen to him without value-judging him in your thoughts. To accept someone means to be understanding of him, because in understanding lies the right appreciation of him. Only then does the right answer or the lawful solution flow from your inner being to you. This means that you become aware of the right answer or solution.

So, when you can accept your neighbor, you will be able to take his words into that part of your spiritual consciousness that you have already developed, that is, which is unburdened and light-filled. When the shadows lying over your divine consciousness are filled with light or even removed, then the light shines through more intensely and you receive a lawful solution. This radiates into those brain cells that you have cleansed and aligned with God, and conveys directly to you the answer for difficulties and problems, and thus, the answers to questions, conversations or letters.

The lawful solution also lies in your homework assignments. We will talk about this later.

And so, you have every lawful solution and answer in yourself, because your inner body is divine, the Absolute Law, itself. They flow to you only when you are *not against* your neighbor, but *for* him.

The Absolute Law has a lawful answer to every question, and the lawful solution for every difficulty and every problem – for everything that happens.

Even in every object there is the positive power, the solution to problems and difficulties related to this object. The lawful solution tells you how you should move, consider, or even use the objects and things.

The developed spiritual consciousness – True wealth – Pray and work – Everything necessary is registered, for example, your lessons – The pure is served by the pure

Dear brother, dear sister, how do you attain the life in God? It is wonderful! I know, because I am this life. You are it, as well!

However, so many people do not know this, since they still judge and condemn, and they move and value-judge everything according to their small, human horizon.

Gradually you realize that within a person there is a mighty *treasure* – of unimaginable extent and spiritual strength. It is the wellspring, and the origin of the wellspring – God. It is the cosmic energy and the origin of the cosmic energy – the primordial light, from which the law for infinity goes out.

In every human being, deep in his soul, lies concealed the whole universe, which consists of the seven basic powers. They are the eternal heavens, our homeland.

Know that this inner treasure remains concealed to *the one* who does not want to unearth it. It can be unearthed only by fulfilling the divine laws; for the treasure is the divine law.

Every spirit being is the entirety, itself. The spiritual body consists of primordial matter, of condensed spiritual energy. It is fine-material and weightless. The whole spiritual body contains all of infinity in compact radiation – that is, as spiritual essence.

This is the greatest gift from the Father-Mother-God, from the divine law; it is the inheritance for His children. Therefore, we all, every single one of us, are heirs to the whole of infinity. It belongs to us just as to our heavenly Father. The entire cosmic radiation, the inheritance, is in us – and thus, in you, too, because your spiritual body is primordial matter from God, and the whole radiation of infinity is active in it, as essence.

Every pure spirit being knows each ray of the complete radiation and can make use of it in a lawful way. Every person whose soul lives in the awareness of God for the most part also knows the eternal law and will behave accordingly. People who are in the law of God for the most part practice tolerance, understanding and selfless love toward those who are still wrestling with their effects.

People in the Spirit of God have inner greatness, for they are in the law of God. They know the lawful answer to each question and the lawful solution in all difficulties and problems as well as in all things and events.

Let us go back to the *energy of the day* again, your good friend. So, each day, each person is guided or controlled differently – depending on the maturity of his soul.

Your teachers, too, are under the influence of the forces of the day. When your teacher is giving a lesson, then do not evaluate the lesson as to whether it is interesting to you or whether you want to hear it or not today. Do not judge your teacher either, if he is not as free and radiant today as he may have been the day before.

Be quiet, just as the divine part in you is quiet. Absorb what is being said and be willing to experience the lawful answer in you.

Concerning this, I, your sister Liobani, want to give you a tip: Follow the lessons attentively, because today you don't yet know whether you might just need some of it already tomorrow! You, the person, do not know – however, your divine consciousness does.

Therefore, practice listening to what is being said, even if it does not really interest you. Whatever you will need for the future, you can deposit in the three memory banks within you: in your *consciousness*, in your *subconscious* – that is, in your brain – and in your *soul garments*, in the particles of your soul. When these repositories are filled with data, you can use them lawfully, now and in the future; and your spiritual consciousness can reflect to you the answer and solution to everything that comes to you from without.

Your spiritual consciousness then gives you help, which is of manifold kinds. Your genes are of importance here as well, for they, too, are influenced by the spiritual consciousness! Your special abilities, qualities and talents are stored there.

The divine in you is always concerned about your well-being. And so, let the lesson flow into you. Accept it – and your divine consciousness will then take it into the three memory banks, in your brain, in your subconscious and in the particles of your soul, so as to reflect to you, tomorrow or in the future, what is lawful, what you should think, speak and do lawfully.

As you have just heard, your developed spiritual consciousness is also linked with your genes, in which lie your abilities, qualities and talents. For your better understanding, I will explain to you:

An *ability* is the skill to carry out something. *Quality* means that what you carry out is work of high quality. *Talents* are gifts that you have brought along, which you develop yourself or with others and with which you design and arrange things.

Your divine consciousness will draw from your classes, from your lesson, *that* which you will need and must know in the future for your profession, and store it in your consciousness, your subconscious and also in your soul. It also helps you to choose your profession, because it knows your abilities, qualities and talents and takes them into consideration.

When you are attentive and participate in class, you will receive from your inner being the right answer to your teacher's questions, because the divine in you transmits the answer and the solution to the understanding, tolerant and selfless child of God. However bear in mind that in order to be able to live in you, in the divine, and to draw and receive from the pure Being, the divine, you first must be mostly pure, yourself! Therefore mark the following words:

Only the pure is served by the pure.

The impure is served by his own kind, by the impure.

The one who relates to external things and is concerned only about his *own* welfare can be used by unlawful energy fields or even by souls, which then can work and live through him. Then, in many situations, such a person is no longer himself, but is controlled and lived.

Therefore, practice self-recognition and strive to neither overrate nor cultivate your base nature, whatever is still human.

Clear up what you have recognized in yourself as human and egocentric aspects! In your prayer, ask Christ for His support and His help, so that you can gain the strength to turn over to Him what you are aware of as being unlawful in yourself – and that you are also able to forgive and ask for forgiveness and have the strength not to make these mistakes any more.

Remember: The pure is served by the pure. The impure by his own kind, by what he is.

A person is as his thoughts, his words and his actions are. They tell how the person really is. When I am speaking of human thoughts, words and actions, I mean what vibrates in the thoughts, in the words and in the actions. This is the person. And so, this is you.

You have heard that a person bears an imperishable treasure in himself. And so, he is richer than he will ever be able to grasp. This has nothing to do with external wealth, but with the spiritual inheritance I mentioned, the wealth of the soul.

Someone who is rich merely externally can still be very poor in his inner being – if he keeps his wealth to himself and strives to increase it for himself, alone. Thus, people who are rich solely in external matters have not yet opened the seal to the inner life and have therefore not yet entered their inner being.

Many people believe that wealth in terms of money and goods is the true life. This is a deception of the senses! True wealth is the *inner* treasure – it is the developed spiritual consciousness. People also call it the "philosopher's stone," which shines in many facets into the person's consciousness and into his subconscious. It is able to guide him and to give and convey to him all he needs and even beyond that.

The one who only hoards money and goods and considers them as his property and is intent on augmenting them for himself does not yet live in the fullness of God. Such people will continue to be poor in their inner being for as long as they are characterized by their human ego – and until they recognize that external wealth is a gift from God to all those who strive for the inner kingdom and follow the divine law of "pray and work."

Note that the rich one received external wealth in order to share it with those who strive for the inner kingdom, creating a basis for those who follow.

Every human being should live according to the law of God. A person who strives for the inner life, the law of God, will, through actualization, also unearth the inner treasure, the treasure of the wise. However, the one who keeps the gifts from God for himself will live in want in one of his next lives on earth in order to feel what it means to be poor in the earthly garment.

This does not mean that a rich person should give away his money and property to simply anyone, but rather, that it should be applied for the welfare of those who endeavor to fulfill the will of God. The Kingdom of God, the kingdom of love and peace, shall come to all people of good will. For this, God has given mankind the commandment "pray and work."

Someone who strives to keep the laws of God in his everyday life, who strives to please God with his work, who neither takes advantage of his fellowman nor exploits him, but sees and acknowledges the positive forces in his neighbor as a spiritual part of his own consciousness, fulfills the law "pray and work" – thereby, he is *for* his neighbor and not against him.

Such a person will selflessly put his money and property to work for the benefit of many without profiting from it. Such people are rich in their inner being. They live in great thoughts and have great thoughts, too. Great thoughts are selfless and not focused on one's own small ego. They are thoughts for the common good, for all people who are of good will.

The inner freedom of the impersonal life – To be servile and to serve – The "puddle law" of the self-centered person – Personal and impersonal speaking

Recognize that a human being should not admire any person or consider him to be superior – not even if he is very rich and esteemed. Pay honor to God alone – and not to a human being. Man should not be servile to any person either, but serve God and mankind.

To be servile means to bow and scrape before a person in order to obtain recognition and reward from him. Know that you do not need to be servile, for a conscientious work is worth its wage.

A person should esteem and respect his neighbor and have a positive attitude toward him; he should not insult or disparage his fellowman, or judge him either, but *serve* him selflessly! He should not, however, pay honor to him and bow before him; this is due to God alone!

You shall not be servile to any person also implies that you shall not tell someone just what he wants to hear, namely that you agree with him, even though you feel and think differently – and ultimately know that his thoughts and his behavior are against the law of God and against the commandment of mutual respect. That would then be servility and hypocrisy.

To pay honor to God means to strive to fulfill God's will.

Live in great thoughts: Strive to be honest and open toward your fellowman; however, do not say out loud everything you think! First, examine your thoughts, whether they are honest and in the will of God.

When they are great, that is, kind, selfless and caring thoughts, then formulate them in such a way that you do not overtax your neighbor and that he does not become agitated or annoyed because he has misunderstood you. Take care to give your neighbor an answer that stimulates him to reflect.

If you spoke in an impersonal way, which means you drew the answer and the solution from that part of your consciousness that is already light-filled, and your neighbor becomes agitated all the same, then you did not burden yourself. You stirred up an already active correspondence, which may possibly cause him to think about it later on. However, if you spoke from your ego and only feigned being impersonal, then you have burdened your soul.

You will quickly realize whether you have received the answer from within, from your light-filled consciousness, or from your person, your conscious mind: If there is the slightest tinge in you of disparaging your neighbor, or human emotions such as envy or condemnation, for instance, then the answer and solution does not come from your mature inner being, but from your intellect, your brain – or partly from within and partly from without. It then is a mixed answer or solution. This means that not all of it has been drawn from the already light-filled part of your consciousness.

If you often act in such a way that you receive part of the answer and solution from within and mix it with your human aspects, then the inner being will gradually grow silent. This means that you cannot receive the answers and solutions from the light-filled part of your consciousness any more because your ego components – the human aspects, that which you have let flow in – have gradually covered up the part of your shining consciousness that is your lawful helper and advisor.

If you live in this conflict, do not say that this is the rightful answer and solution. First examine your behavior toward your neighbor!

You have read: The pure is served by the pure. The pure in you is the divine, the eternal law, God. Only the one who has cleared his soul for the most part receives the pure.

The more the divine consciousness unfolds, that is, expands, in you, the more powers of light and divine information flow to you.

The answer and the solution from the irradiated part of your consciousness is not only the Inner Helper and Advisor for your neighbor, but also gives you, day by day, the lawful information for your own life, for your work and thought. What radiates to you from your shining consciousness is *impersonal* – all the information for your life, the answer and solution for your neighbor or the question to your neighbor. It is the impersonal life that answers you.

The impersonal life communicates to *the* soul and *the* person who strive to live impersonally – which means you do not treat your neighbor personally by, for example, thinking or saying: "You're wicked, you're unqualified, you're lazy, you're a bad person, you're wrong, you're a liar," or the like. All this is personal, and thus, human.

You are impersonal if you respect and appreciate your neighbor as a child of God, when you do not judge or condemn him, but search for and find the good in him and affirm it.

This does not mean that you should take no notice of his faults and weaknesses. Through his light-filled consciousness, the impersonal person is able to address his neighbor's faults in an impersonal manner. This means to draw his attention to his faults without agitation and without mixing in his own human ego.

However, when you approve of your neighbor's human aspects and flatter him although you realize that it is not right, and you do so only in order to be praised by him, then you are personal and will burden yourself.

Personal and self-centered is also *the* person who remains silent when his neighbor is treated unjustly and is condemned. The one who recognizes this and nevertheless remains silent becomes guilty – because by his silence he agrees with the injustice. To remain silent so as not to become unpopular is, like many other things, personal: The person wants to safeguard his ego and not vouch for his neighbor. And so, when you realize that injustice is being done and you keep quiet, you make yourself an accessory to it.

Again, be aware that everything that comes from God, from the light-filled, the opened part of your consciousness, is impersonal. The impersonal does not force a person to do this or that. It only elucidates and explains. This is why what I reveal to you from the Spirit of God bears the title: I Explain – Will You Join Me?

The impersonal does not *forbid* anything to you, but rather *bids* you. God gave free will to all His children. This is why the Eternal bids us, so that His children, who have stepped outside the eternal law, will find their way back. *When* they will again live within the light of the freedom of the cosmic being is determined by each individual, himself.

Someone who does not keep the law of God creates his own law. It consists of his human thoughts and desires. Everything that a person does from his personal ego is against

God and against the eternal law of freedom. With this, the person binds himself to his own thoughts, ideas and desires, which he thus affirms and which, exert influence on him, in turn. He lives in this law of his own creation – and it, in turn, affects him.

We can call this law of the ego the "personal law" or also the *"puddle law."* It is the law of cause and effect: What a person sows, he will reap.

In this puddle law, the so-called thought-bacteria accumulate. They bring illness, blows of fate and they bring back what the person has sown, for example, hatred, envy and hostility. If the person is spiteful, he sows hatred; if he envies his neighbor's belongings, he sows envy; if he lives in discord with his neighbor, he sows hostility – and he will reap, in turn, accordingly. Wars can possibly emerge from this.

All of this is the so-called puddle law, the law of cause and effect: The person spun himself into his own negative thoughts and his urging, unrealizable desires, like a cocoon. They affect him and bring about in him what he has sown.

With hatred, envy, hostility and the like, the person wastes his life energy. Through this, his organs weaken. After that, the causes take their effect, as illness in the body or as a blow of fate – all according to what the person has sown. It is his own self-made law that affects him.

A person will continue to live in the ruts of his own thinking and wishing, which are *his* law, until he accepts and actualizes the laws of God. Then he will find his way out of his puddle law, out of need, suffering, restriction, affliction, out of the ruts of his thoughts and desires, toward the cosmic freedom of life.

And so, you can keep the commandments or leave them. You have your free will to make a free decision: for the eternal law of freedom or for your own law.

The law of freedom brings independence, beauty, strength, love, warmth, peace and eternal life in God. Your own law gives you what you have input into yourself.

And so, the impersonal life is a life in compliance with the laws of the love and the freedom of God. The impersonal respects the free will of its neighbor. Take note: It *respects* a person's will; it does not affirm it if it is against the divine law. Everything that comes from God is absolute freedom. Since God gave His children their free will as inheritance, He respects what His human children do – yet, He does not reinforce their unlawful behavior.

Now I ask you: What do you want?

Do you want the inner freedom? Then fulfill the commandments and become impersonal!

Do you want to build up your little ego? Then you create your own puddle law and in this puddle, you will live a puddle life. Thought-bacteria and thought-viruses – whatever you have sown – then influence you.

When you keep the commandments, you gradually become impersonal and draw more and more from the inner wellspring, the expanding divine consciousness in you. Then you are free, vigorous, energetic, and thus, impersonal and are led directly by the eternal law, God – and not controlled by your "puddle law!"

Then it is possible for you to follow your lessons in school in a clear and concentrated manner and you will receive from your Inner Helper and Advisor the answers to questions that you can then express.

The Inner Helper and Advisor is the light-filled consciousness in you. You have freed Him from the veils of your human ego. He now stands by you in your school assignments and exams. He also helps you choose the right profession and to be successful in it to the extent that it is beneficial for the common good, for your neighbor. Moreover, He helps you to fulfill your day's task – and even more than that.

Through you, your Inner Helper and Advisor enables you to conduct impersonal conversations and negotiations. He also helps you to write letters.

The impersonal, the light-filled consciousness, is the divine in you. You are God's child, who comes from the pure, eternal Being, and draws from the eternal truth, the wellspring of life.

You have now realized that the eternal light dwells in you. When you turn to the eternal light and actualize what I have commented on from the various facets of the truth, then you will live consciously in God.

Your true being is the pure, fine-material body that lives and works in your physical body. It is cosmic. The more light intensity your consciousness, your spiritual body, is able to radiate, because the veils of your ego have dissolved, the more precise and all-encompassing is the information from within.

So, if you have matured spiritually to the extent that your divine being is able to guide you, it will also be capable of sup porting you in exams and in accomplishing your tasks.

Many a person might now think: "Wonderful, then I no longer have to learn anything, or work any more, either. I will purify my soul – then I will have the right answer and a good solution for everything. With this, I can earn a living."

It is not that simple! First of all, such an attitude would be human and thus, against the law of God. And secondly, God gave man the commandment "pray and work."

Know that the one who goes out of the law of God shall earn his bread by the work of his hands – with his law, which he created himself and from which came forth matter and condensation. Condensation, matter, came into being through the law that the Fall-beings created themselves: the law of cause and effect. All condensed forms emerged through the Fall, because beings were against the laws of God.

Intellect and intelligence – The mind as an instrument of the divine intelligence – The human brain's limited receptivity – The narrowed consciousness of the intellectual person

Let me briefly explain how the human body developed:

A very long time ago, when the earth was still part-material, it was inhabited by beings who were against God. Because of their behavior, they became denser and denser, just as the earth grew coarser, that is, more and more coarse-material – until it became matter, thus, totally dense.

This happened because the *sensations* of these beings became increasingly unlawful, then, later on, their *thinking,* and over the course of their condensation, their *acting,* too, became unlawful.

The condensation of their spiritual bodies began with their heads: That is where a spiritual particle first turned into a cell, that is, into a brain cell. From this one brain cell, further cells developed via cell division, which gradually formed the human body, the shell of the spiritual body. The brain cells absorbed the negative programming, the sensations to work against God and for one's own ego.

And so, know that the human body originated via the head, via the gradually forming brain mass, the brain cells. Condensation started with the head and from the head emerged the first program for the human body. This process of transformation took a very, very long time. I have only given you a rough draft of it. It is not so important to know about this.

What is essential is that you orient yourself to God and illuminate your soul with the power of Christ, so you can become divine again.

Recognize that what happened at the time of the emergence of human beings takes place in a similar way today, as well: A person inputs into his *brain* his ideas and opinions, that is, his human programs – but also his spiritual, lawful programs. All programs then enter the *subconscious* and the spiritual *particles* of the soul from which, in turn, they radiate and form the *soul garments*. A person calls these stored inputs in the brain the *mind* or the *intellect*.

Many people think that when they have stored a great deal of knowledge they are intelligent. Certainly, they have an intellect that has been imprinted accordingly, however, not with true intelligence! *Intelligence* is God's wisdom; it is the life of the All, the universe, because God is the All-consciousness.

The intelligence, God, wants to establish communication with the purified brain cells that are aligned with Him, and thus, work with them. Then the intellect – the brain cells – serves as an instrument through which God reveals Himself in this world and works in this world.

And so, when the human brain, the mind of a person, is aligned with God and the brain cells have stored the lawful principles, then the person is intelligent, because his intellect serves the divine intelligence. Through this, the person becomes an instrument of the divine law on this earth.

Take note: People with "common sense" are people who have placed their thinking and acting in service of the cosmic intelligence. They are the true servants and helpers of mankind. They are people of cosmic intelligence. They draw from and give from their opened consciousness.

When God wants to be effective in this world, He needs people who align their way of thinking and living with Him. For this, a person should know the divine laws and store them in his brain. Then he can work according to the divine laws, for the abilities and talents that lie in his genes become active.

He is then an instrument of the cosmic intelligence. This means that his way of living and working has become a prayer. The person works in the world according to the cosmic laws. He thinks, speaks and works cosmically – this means that his life proceeds according to the eternal laws, according to the law "pray and work."

An intellectual person is mostly concerned with himself; an intelligent person has more spirit power, because he receives from the intelligence, God.

For your better understanding, I repeat: A person is *intellectual* when he merely piles up knowledge, offers it in combination with his human ego and puts it at his own service to gain the means and titles necessary for him. He has not aligned his brain mass with the divine law and thus, does not serve the divine intelligence, the divine wisdom. An intellectual's sole concern is that honor and praise are bestowed on him.

A person aligned with God, an *intelligent* person, renders honor, praise and glory to the eternal intelligence, because he knows that his strength and wisdom come from the eternal intelligence, from God.

The one who programs his brain cells, his intellect, with knowledge alone can only become an intellectual. Intellectual people are often very limited, because the person's brain cells have only a limited capacity to absorb human knowledge. The intellectual can give only what he has stored himself as intellectual knowledge. However, a brain is designed to absorb far more information beyond that.

You read correctly: far more information! By this, I mean the information of the selfless Inner Helper and Advisor, the information of your divine consciousness, the divine intelligence in you.

A person oriented to without is able to activate only a meager part of his brain cells, because he uses up a lot of his own physical energy for his intellectual, self-centered life. In the process, his brain mass becomes overexerted. Therefore, he is receptive only to a limited degree and registers only what his senses are capable of absorbing.

Whoever, relies solely on his physical energy, and can make use of it only because he does not strive for the divine intelligence, is the one whose brain tires very quickly. Practically automatically, the person then confines himself to the spheres of knowledge concerning this side of life.

You have surely experienced yourself that when you are very, very tired, you can still read, for example; yet sooner or later, the time comes when you suddenly notice that you were reading, but no longer know *what* you were reading! This means that your physical energy still gave you strength to read – but your brain wasn't able to register what you read, anymore.

You can experience the same in hearing, smelling, tasting and touching. You may well hear something, and despite this, not know what you heard. You have only a faint notion of what was said, but you can no longer repeat it. This means that your brain cells couldn't store anything more. For this reason, you cannot recall anything from them. About what you smelled and tasted, too, you are unable to furnish any information, because your brain is no longer capable of storing smell and taste impressions.

And so, you can see, hear, smell, taste and touch without being aware of it. Your brain will store a correspondingly small amount.

If, however, you are alert and use your five senses consciously, your brain will also store much of it. For the thoughts that you have while seeing, hearing, smelling, tasting and touching, then go into your brain as inputs.

Your thoughts can be received only by active brain cells, not by inactive ones. Thus, the person can recall solely what he has stored previously.

I repeat: If your body has given you only vestiges of energies to see, hear, smell, taste and touch and if your brain was too tired to absorb what the senses registered, then what the senses took in was stored only in part or not at all. This means that when you work only with your intellect, you may very well go through and experience a lot in your life, but your brain can store only a limited amount of information, since the body tires quickly.

People who live solely in the world and do not develop their inner life, their divine aspects, store essential and unessential matters in their brain cells. By this, too, they quickly overburden their brain cells. Moreover, the potential of that part of the brain mass provided for the absorption of human knowledge is limited. This means those cells are possibly programmed and filled very quickly with essential and unessential matters.

And so, the one who confines himself to the knowledge of this side of life has only a narrow horizon and can store far less in his brain than the intelligent person. If the person has exhausted his brain capacity, that is to say, if the brain is filled with knowledge from this side of life, the person thinks he is wise. People who have only a one-sided orientation, that is, who have stored in their brain only human concerns, knowledge of this side of life, are not wise people, for intellectual knowledge is far from being wisdom. That is why they are also referred to as intellectuals.

This is why you frequently hear from the Spirit of God that intellectuals, matter-of-fact people, are quite limited. This means that their divine consciousness is restricted, as they are not using it, but use only their intellectual knowledge.

The doctors and scientists of this world have recognized that the brain mass could store far more information. They call the part of the brain that lies latent in many, the "unutilized gray cells."

Regarding this, I would like to explain that a major part of the brain mass, the brain cells, is designated exclusively for communication with the divine, the eternal intelligence. This part of the brain cannot be filled by our human thinking, speaking and acting.

Someone, who wants to vivify his brain mass and to awaken many brain cells must first make an effort to recognize the divine laws and then to actualize them. Gradually, communication will set in between the opened divine consciousness and the brain cells that are aligned with the eternal intelligence, which, seen from the human point of view, cannot be programmed. For this large part of the brain mass is intended for the divine intelligence and not the intellect.

Whoever actualizes the divine laws attains the training of the heart. He lives in great thoughts. He respects and cherishes his fellowman, is understanding of him, is tolerant and favorably inclined toward them.

People of the Spirit will not be a party to human aspects that violate the divine law. People with great thoughts do not judge or condemn. They leave their fellowman his free will. They strive to fulfill the will of God despite all the misunderstandings they frequently encounter.

Someone who strives to live in great thoughts is also able to put his thoughts in order, to curb his language and to master his senses. This attitude enables him to fully concentrate on a matter and to follow his school lessons attentively already as a young person. Such people are not scatter-brained, for they live in great thoughts and do not distract themselves with non-essential, little, human ego-thoughts nor do they let these distract them.

The one who lives in such an attitude of mind comes in contact with the Inner Helper and Advisor, the divine intelligence, the light-filled consciousness. Then, what I already mentioned will take place: The consciousness stores, for example, what the student will need now or in the future from the lesson. For the consciousness knows the soul and the nature of the person's genes and knows what will be stored and activated in them – or what can be activated during this earthly existence.

Understanding, good will, tolerance and their limits – Ties resulting from expectations – The straightforward and selflessly helping ones

Once more, let me refer to understanding, tolerance and good will and, from further facets of the divine truth, throw light on these three aspects which should be applied in the causal law:

People who strive to keep the commandments of God show understanding and good will for their fellowman in whatever situation he may find himself and are tolerant toward everybody. However, they will not join those who intend something unlawful or demand it of them. They remain within the divine commandments, which are given for the earth from the law of God.

To show *understanding* means to understand your neighbor and to also stand by him and help him according to the law of God – but not to fortify his ego or even do what he – contrary to the divine law – wants to gain by force.

The same is true of *good will*. People expecting good will want an advantage for their well-being, personally. They want what appears to be agreeable and useful to them. A spiritual person will even tolerate these expectations – and he will also support his neighbor insofar as it corresponds to the law of God and to his neighbor's efforts to find his way out of a difficult situation on his own initiative.

Someone who strives to fulfill the will of God will not submit to a person's will and do what the latter demands for his own human well-being. Whoever carries out what the self-centered person wants of him puts himself on this person's level of life and milieu and lets himself be controlled by this person. Through this, he becomes dependent on the self-centered person and binds himself to the world of the other's desires and thoughts.

Dependency also occurs at our place of work. However here, the reality is different; the point in question here is the work, the execution of the work and staying on schedule. At his place of work everyone should behave as is required of him by his employment contract. The employment contract contains the rights and duties of both employer and employee.

Let the word *tolerance* take effect in you and absorb its vibrations; then you will understand the following:

To tolerate means not to reject your neighbor's mindset, even if he moves at the edges of the law or even wades in the morass of matter. To tolerate also means not to want to change your neighbor with your human ego. Explain to him impersonally about his wrong doing. However, do not force him to think and act differently. Everyone has his free will to shape his life as he wants – and he alone has to account for his life before God and himself, based on the law of sowing and reaping.

To tolerate does not mean that you should do the same or like thing. If, for example, you realize that your neighbor's behavior is against the divine law and despite knowing better, you do the same or like thing, then you put yourself into his milieu and are bound to him. Fulfill your neighbor's desires only to a degree and only when you recognize that through this he will come to his senses and not make the same mistakes again.

Many people choose the easy way out when it comes to helping their fellowman. Frequently they fulfill his self-centered desires and give in to his self-will – only for the sake of peace or to look good.

They reinforce his human aspects, even though they realize that in doing so they can either help him not at all or only for a short while – until he again expresses the same desires and expects, in turn, that his will is done. In this case, helping has nothing to do with understanding, good will or tolerance!

The one who supports and backs his neighbor's self-will expects to be supported by him, as well. He expects either recognition or reward. Through this, both lean on each other and expect the same from each other: that the other fulfill what seems good and helpful to the one. This means that both are bound to each other and burden themselves before the law of God. Through the law of sowing and reaping, they will remain bound to each other until they both undo what they caused by their wrong behavior.

Recognize that the one who binds himself to people relies on people. Whoever relies on people cleaves to his human ego. He sees things and events only from *his own* perspective and will expect – just as the one he is bound to – understanding, good will and tolerance from the other.

Those who expect something lack what they expect – and they do not want to work for it either: They expect their neighbor to do or achieve what they have not developed themselves, what they do not possess, themselves.

Someone who supports this attitude of expectation in his fellowman, by fulfilling the latter's desires, by affirming his views, which means that he does what is expected of him, is on the same track as the one who expects, because he expects, as well.

People who constantly keep declaring their expectations are neither able to understand nor accept those who neither affirm their attitude of expectation, nor agree with their opinions and therefore, do not fulfill their will. This is why they disparage those who do not give in to their desires or confirm their opinions, because they receive no aggrandizement from those who remain straightforward – that is, they receive no endorsement for themselves, for what *they* think, want or do.

Therefore, the one who remains straightforward often has to endure judgment and condemnation, thus experiencing the aggressions of those whose expectations were not fulfilled or endorsed. Straightforward people are often the target for those who do not want to take their life into their own hands and master it. And so, whoever practices understanding, good will and tolerance, yet does not fulfill those human aspects his neighbor expects, will always be exposed to a bombardment of negative thoughts from the other side.

And so, if you aspire to straightforwardness, remember that the darkling, who wants to keep you in the law of sowing and reaping, will fight against you in sensations and thoughts.

Therefore, beware of any speculations and compromises such as fulfilling your neighbor's will for the sake of peace. If you think: "I'll flatter him now or do his will, so I can go my way or have my peace," then this is already the first step into dependency.

The one who is or becomes dependent can be influenced and cannot make a clear decision anymore in situations resulting from his dependency. Such people then speak and act out of their dependency and accuse their fellowman who does not fulfill what they ask for. They then accuse him of his lack of understanding, his intolerance and unkindness.

Pay attention to your sensations, whether they are divine! You can figure them out correctly only when you are honest and sincere with yourself and put yourself on the side of the eternal law, which is selfless love, kindness and gentleness. And so, strive to keep the commandments and you will attain constancy in God.

Know that the one who enters into the law of love for God, by actualizing the commandments of love and by discarding the human aspects, is filled with selfless love. From selfless love flow kindness and gentleness. In the world, among human beings, kindness and gentleness are transformed into patience and mercy. And the one who is filled with patience and mercy is sincere and steadfast.

People who are filled with selfless love help and serve, so that those who expect and accuse may recognize themselves in this. However, they remain steadfast and will not – as people might say – "howl with the wolves," since they are not waiting for prey.

You have now heard several things concerning the deep meaning of the words understanding, good will and tolerance.

The consciousness in you, the Inner Helper and Advisor – Receiving answers and finding solutions, for example, in your homework – Conscientious and selfless behavior results in well-being

I, Liobani, your sister from the spiritual home, will now continue my explanations concerning the issue of receiving answers and finding solutions.

You have heard that it is important to be attentive in class. If you absorb the lessons conscientiously, then you will also do your homework well and pass the tests and exams in a way that is good for you and your continuing life on earth. When you are attentive, thus preparing your brain cells accordingly, your light-filled consciousness will store your lessons in your soul particles – and later, when it becomes necessary, it can transmit the right answer and solution to you. You thereby store in your brain cells the meaning of the lesson as well, and, at the same time, the corresponding words that you need to express yourself clearly.

A person who is with God is in God, and God accomplishes His work through him. This means that God, the light-filled consciousness in you, your Inner Helper and Advisor, gives you the right answers and solutions in your sensations and thoughts.

To be with God does not mean to be bigoted, nor does it mean to affect piety and solely meditate. To be with God and in God means to radiate love, kindness and gentleness and to show understanding, tolerance and good will toward your neighbor. However, as you have already learned, this does not imply supporting your neighbor's self-will and thereby making yourself a slave to his will and desires.

To be in and with God means to stand in the world and to correctly fulfill the tasks you have taken on; to support, help and serve those people who need help and service – but not to be servile or to help merely in order to be left in peace or to receive a service in return.

Nor should you be servile at your place of work. Strive each day to conscientiously do the work assigned to you; then you will earn corresponding wages, for every just worker is due his wage.

There are many opportunities every day to be selfless toward your fellowman! At your place of work, too, you should keep the law of serving and of selfless help. During your work, with which you earn your bread, you should think, live and act as God wants: being kind, understanding, merciful, tolerant, of good will and ready to help.

Wherever somebody has been placed in his life on earth, he is the architect of his own fate. There, he can actualize what was given to him as a program for this life on earth – or instead burden himself anew, thus setting the course for his future lives on earth, if he does not follow the law of free will concerning all people and if he does not dedicate his life to the law of love, kindness, mercy, good will and understanding.

And be conscientious in the activities you do to earn your living! Remain selfless whether you earn money for a living or whether you are at school or at home with your parents or with friends. Give help selflessly where help is needed and radiate kindness and good will, without thereby supporting your neighbor's self-will.

According to the law of love, things will go well for the one who strives for the divine law of love and freedom and actualizes it. This means that he will not suffer need; he will receive help in illness or he will master his life on earth without illness.

With this, I mean the lawful well-being of which the Spirit of Christ speaks: Practice selfless love, so that things go well for you on earth, so that you thus have little or nothing to endure or suffer. Every selfless activity is supported by the divine wisdom – which is also called the divine deed.

What a student has to do also belongs to these activities. You are still a student and it is your task to learn, that is, to program your brain cells with the data you will need for your future life on earth. Therefore, concentrate in school when a lesson is given. Then you can also concentrate on your schoolwork and solve it in a good and satisfactory way.

Before you start with your homework, sit down quietly and in an upright way. Close your eyes for a moment and turn your senses and thoughts inward to God, your and our Lord and Father, and ask the eternal love, God, the eternal law, for help. The request for support and help activates the light-filled consciousness in you.

This short closing of your eyes and turning to God, the eternal Intelligence, the Advisor and Helper in you, goes unnoticed. If it is noticed, then stand up for it! Do not disavow God – no matter what others think or say.

After this short turn inward, open your eyes again and look at the task before you. This means that you consciously take in the reading material, the math formulas or whatever else is a part of the assignment. By doing this, you establish communication with that part of your activated spiritual consciousness that is unburdened for the most part and is able to reach your consciousness. This results in communication between the divine in you – your Inner Helper and Advisor – and yourself, the person aspiring to God, your consciousness.

Then the divine in you radiates more strongly into the brain cells in which this subject is stored and also touches the correct words for it. The inner light, the divine intelligence, connects knowledge and words in your brain. This process arrives at your consciousness as sensations and thoughts – and suddenly, you know the solution for your assignment.

This task as well as further tasks, which you take into yourself, already bears within the answer and the solution. And the answers and solutions are in your light-filled consciousness, for the divine knows all things. You, however, have to establish a connection to the divine, that is, establish communication with the divine intelligence.

Know that just as the answer and solution are already in the schoolwork, that is how they are in all questions, problems and difficulties.

Recognize that communication with the divine in you is, however, possible only when the corresponding lesson has been learned and stored in your brain cells. Only then, can the divine cast light on these cells.

However, the Inner Helper and Advisor cannot radiate to your brain cells unimpeded, and you cannot receive him when you are preoccupied with difficulties and problems. Through this, you condense the cloudiness, the shadows, that are superimposed over your light-filled consciousness.

This is why it is indispensable for you to live consciously, which means, if possible, to clear up at once difficulties and problems that come up, so that you are not clouded over. Even human thoughts – anything that does not comply with the law of God – you should always immediately surrender to the Spirit of Christ, your Redeemer in you, so that He may transform them into positive power.

Regarding this, a comparable image: When the sky is cloudy, the rays of the sun cannot shine to the earth unimpeded. If the cloudiness were permanent, vegetation and people would suffer. Nature would gradually become stunted and the human body would grow ill. If it constantly rained, the soil would become over-acidified and the fruits of the gardens and fields could not ripen. They would rot already in the seed, along with the half-ripe fruits on the trees.

It is similar with those people who cling to their difficulties and problems and constantly speak about them. The difficulties and problems are the clouds, the shadows which overlay the light-filled consciousness.

The one who is preoccupied only with his difficulties and problems is also unable to make use of the energy of the day and does not understand what the day wants to tell him and bring him.

And when you think about your fellowman and talk negatively about him, you cannot make use of the day. The day passes you by and takes its gifts and help away with it again.

What you have not recognized and thus, not cleared up on this very day will be brought again by another day – perhaps in an intensified form as grief and suffering, because you increased the negative aspects in you through your continued wrong way of thinking.

Through your teachers, as well, the day's energy wants to tell you something of what you should recognize and learn today. In the same way, your homework is a task for you that comes from the energy of the day.

If you are inattentive in school while the lesson is being taught, if you are preoccupied with other things or with your fellowman, then you establish no link to your light-filled consciousness. It is then unable to contact your brain cells, in which the essentials of the lesson were to be absorbed. In this case, your light-filled consciousness, the divine intelligence in you, cannot convey to you the answers and solutions for your homework, nor can it in the future, because you have not set up any communication program in your brain cells.

Therefore, take in the school lessons conscientiously – you never know if and when you will need them for your continuing life!

As long as you are a human being, your light-filled consciousness needs your brain cells as communication instruments; for it is via them that it conveys its information to you. If your brain cells are stuffed full of difficulties, problems and nonessential things, then you cannot perceive an echo, a resonance, and this means no answers and no solutions for your tasks. For your brain is the sounding-board for your light-filled, divine consciousness.

If you did not follow the lesson, because you were preoccupied with other things and could not keep your thoughts on the explanations of the tasks, then your divine consciousness cannot help you, the person, nor can it store anything in your brain or then convey anything to you as an answer or solution.

This is why it is important that you not dwell too long on trifles and that you quickly settle difficulties and problems.

A person's free will – The path to constant contact with the consciousness in us, to true intelligence and wisdom: principles, criteria and instructions

To be clear means to be ready to absorb.

People who rest in themselves and are one with God have a clear mind. They are clear thinkers. They instantly grasp things and have the right, that is, the lawful, solution right away! How come? Because there are no dark shadows cast over their spiritual consciousness, that is, their horizon is not clouded over. The rays of the inner sun reach the active brain cells unhindered, which store what the person is.

You will now ask: "What is a human being?"

The human being is energy, thus radiation! We can also say that he is a bundle of energy or a bundle of rays. The person, the bundle of energy, the radiation, consists of what is already predetermined in the person's genes and of what he thinks day after day, that is, what he absorbs and stores.

What lies in the genes is also stored in the soul's particles, and radiates out via the soul's garments. For a soul only enters a body that has a similar vibration. The radiation of the soul and the radiation of the genes are identical for the most part.

A person has free will. Day by day, he decides anew what he intends to make of his life. The soul may very well influence the person via his genes, but the person himself decides what to make of it: a free, selfless life or a life that vegetates away and is a captive of its own fate.

To influence means to have something flow in. This means that whatever is stored in the soul and in the genes flows into the person's life, into his world of thoughts.

Now it is up to the person what kind of thoughts he decides for: for human thoughts, which are against God – or for divine thoughts, which bring him a light-filled, free and healthy life.

A person's external appearance is marked by his soul – in connection with his genes and his world of thoughts. These will also control his aspirations and strivings, his decision for the good or for the evil.

In every situation of life in which the person has to decide, he receives God's help: It is effective via the *conscience,* into which your guardian spirit also gives impulses. It communicates via fine and gentle sensations that inspire you to think of the good and to react and act selflessly. It can also communicate with you through a conversation with your neighbor or via occurrences in the day.

At every instant, it is possible to decide and to *turn back,* as every instant contains God's help and God's power. The eternal spirit in a human being, the guardian spirit and the energy of the day are admonishers, helpers and servants of a person, so that he may recognize in time his wrongdoing as a cause, and clear it up before the fate he himself has created strikes.

God's love guides His child in manifold ways and strives to lead it in time out of the causes it created itself.

Our heavenly Father is love and wants to free you from all burdens, so that your horizon may broaden and become light-filled and you can absorb His power of love, His wisdom and greatness without hindrance. With the help of our heavenly Father, you can clear up all that hinders you to think clearly or to become wise.

Recognize: The whole of infinity is the logos; it is God. The whole of infinity is intelligence, is wisdom of God.

Take these principles to heart:

- Put your thoughts in order! Then your life will become ordered.
- Give up your self-will. Do not lead anyone by his nose – do not deprive him of his free will.
- Practice finding the good in all people. Then you will also respect their free will and become free, yourself, of prejudice, opinions and bindings.
- Actualize the spiritual knowledge you have stored. Then your horizon will become clear, and you will be able to receive the cosmic intelligence, the divine wisdom. Then your light-filled consciousness will communicate with you – no matter where you are or what you do. For the universal intelligence, the divine wisdom, is in you.

Now you will grasp more and more easily the difference between intelligence and intellect. What do you want: intelligence or intellect? It is up to you!

You now know that the universal intelligence is in you and that only you can come into communication with it, yourself – your neighbor cannot do this for you.

I, Liobani, will now explain to my brothers and sisters in the earthly garment how they should behave in order to be in continuous contact with their spiritual body, their spiritual consciousness, the divine intelligence:

Dear brother, dear sister, plant deep in your inner being the certainty that you are a spiritual being in an earthly garment, which is served by every cosmic ray. The human being, the outer body, is merely the shell in which the spirit being is found.

Become aware that the spirit being in you has infinite powers that work untiringly. The person is able to address them only after having removed the veils of his human ego from his soul. A conscious life is the requirement for this.

In order to be able to live in and also draw from your inner being, your true being, your light-filled spiritual consciousness, you should learn *to be reflective*.

Do not be a chatterbox, a person who expresses anything that comes to mind. Become a thoughtful, prudent person! You can activate this quality – in whatever situation you may be in – by remembering your true nature: It is loving, kind and conscious of its inner strength.

If in every situation you recall in this way the infallible, lawful power of love in you, then from the depth of your inner being, from the opened part of your consciousness, you will receive the lawful answer and solution to all your tasks, questions, difficulties and problems – or find the way for the right action.

The true being within you is your spiritual body that came from the heavens; it is on earth to serve those who still need help, who have still learned little or nothing about their true being.

And through me, Liobani, you are called upon by your heavenly Father, who is also my Father, to unfold the eternal forces, so that you may find your way out of misery, anxiety and despair – and are also able to show your fellowman the way out of the narrow confines of fear, despair and egoism.

In order to become wise, that is, intelligent, heed the following:

Do not brag about your knowledge! This is not nice and is no indication of sagacity – let alone wisdom.

Try to fulfill my indications; above all, purify your soul by refining your human thoughts and the still ignoble senses.

Moreover, you can *try out* what I have revealed to you; then you can find out how it works in yourself and in your surroundings – also at school.

However, I ask you: Do *not talk* about what you are trying out or what you have already succeeded in, but rather: become, grow and mature!

To become, grow and mature means to become more and more aware of the fact that you are a child of God and harbor in your inner being inconceivable spiritual treasures. If you want to unearth them, you must first gain access to your inner being.

Apply good characteristics, such as tolerance, understanding and good will, and increasingly grow into the divine law, which you then fulfill – and which fills you. This is how spiritual growth takes place. From growth ensues spiritual maturity. Through the fulfillment of the laws, you become the true fruit: You unearth the treasure of your inner being and are *wise*.

Then you will not explain to your fellowman how wise you are or that you have become wise; a wise man does not boast! He does not throw his weight around. A wise person talks little, but in a frank and clear way. He *is*. This means he radiates the truth. What he says is profound in content, which flows from the inner wisdom.

His attitude toward his fellowmen is of good will, yet not obtrusive. He helps and gives where it is appropriate. What he accomplishes, he does selflessly. Wise, that is, truly intelligent, people are kind, active and alert.

A truly wise man does not see merely the external appearance, the mannerisms and the talk of people. He looks deep into their inner being and recognizes how they are. Truly wise people look at the essential and do not converse about unessential matters.

People of the Spirit live from within and also give from within, from their true being, from the spiritual body in the physical body. They draw from their light-filled consciousness, which is their spiritual body.

To be able to give from your second, your eternal, body, you must first find your way to it. Therefore, as far as the first steps on your way to your true being, to your eternal body are concerned, the following applies: Find yourself! No one else can eat and digest for you. And no one else can find and unearth the inner treasure, your true being, for you. Only you, yourself!

Therefore, strive to go into your inner being by removing in the right way all obstacles erected by the human ego. Then you will become wise, intelligent.

To find your way to your own self, you must go within more and more; this means, to live the day and not be lived by the day! If you accomplish this, you will recognize very soon that you can carry out many things of the day quickly and successfully.

Your *journal,* too, in which you note down everything – your daily exercises, what needs to be cleared up or what you have already fulfilled – helps you to recognize and find yourself.

Also note in your journal the way you develop contact to your light-filled consciousness and how the impulses and the communication arrive at your conscious mind.

The notes in your journal are little aids and let you realize that you are maturing spiritually, that you live the day and are not lived by it.

Through your connection to your inner being, your light-filled consciousness, your schoolwork will also turn out to your teacher's satisfaction, and you will pass the exams at school much more easily. You will know yourself that you have done your homework correctly. You will pass the exams on your school subjects not just with an average grade; even "good" and "excellent" marks will not be missing.

Know that the light-filled person is served by his true being, his light-filled consciousness.

The help of God is very close to you, when you make use of the days, that is, when you surrender yourself and the day to God first thing in the morning; when you ask for His guidance and help, and when during the day you keep reminding yourself that God stands by you when you do what is necessary for this: When, during the day, you repeatedly turn to within in prayer and also enter into your journal what you were successful in doing and where you failed.

Again and again, remember your light-filled consciousness and be sure that the Spirit of our heavenly Father wants to help you at all times. Go into the stillness not only in the morning, but also at noon and in the evening, so that you keep up the connection to God.

To go into stillness means: Sit upright, close your eyes and turn to within to the Spirit of God in you.

Only in stillness is becoming, growing and maturing possible. Become still and surrender yourself to God, so that the divine wisdom may grow out of you and bring forth its fruits.

To become still does not mean you should distance yourself from sports and games or even from your fellowman and your schoolmates! Wise people do not dissociate themselves from their fellowman. They live among them as shining examples. People who stay in contact with God's love and wisdom are not peculiar. And so, join the games that appeal to you from within, and go on bicycle tours or car excursions, if you enjoy them.

Be just in all things, however, do not argue in order to be right. Do not justify yourself when it is a question of who is right. Clear things up, that means: Put right what is wrong – whether you gain approval or not. Be the young person who is understanding and kind in every situation.

Know that within you is the just Spirit, which knows about every situation and masters it. It sees things and events as they are, not as they seem to be at the moment.

Do not expect God to intervene when you think it is the right time. The divine in you knows when justice will be done to you. So leave the right time to God.

He will disclose the injustice *then*, when the one who has committed injustice is also able to learn from it. Therefore, trust in His justice in all things.

Never be sulky or quarrelsome. This is all-too-human. People who live more in the Spirit of God, and are not solely concerned with material matters, are not offended. They are not quarrelsome either, because they do not insist they are right.

They live in great thoughts, that is, they are selfless, kind, understanding and benevolent toward every person. They see people and things as they are and not as they seem to the offended or quarrelsome one.

Learn to look into every situation. Then you will become wise. For you already know that every situation, even a dispute, already contains the spiritual answer or solution.

Restrain yourself in every situation – and link with your Inner Helper and Advisor. If it is good, He will give you the answer or solution via your inner being, and then you can bring it up as a help. However, you must not deprive your neighbor of his free will!

But be aware that your answer or your solution do not have to be accepted by the quarrelsome or offended parties. Offer the answer or the solution merely as a help.

Do not boast by announcing out loud where you have the answer or the solution from! Stay wise – give help only when you are asked for help. Never impose yourself or your help!

Recognize: It is not you, the person, who are wise, but the divine consciousness in you is the wisdom, the selfless, wise life!

You can monitor your own spiritual development and maturity when you live consciously each day and keep your journal conscientiously. Then you recognize the stages of your spiritual development and maturity, and you experience yourself again and again. Take time every evening to bring your day and your journal to a close and to make the carry-over to the next day's page: What has been settled and what still remains to be cleared up in the way of human aspects. Through this you are in control of your thinking, speaking and acting. You know what you have already overcome and what you are still working on. You yourself recognize your highs and lows, your failures and your spiritual progress.

When you keep your journal in a conscientious way and every evening bring it to a close and make the carry-over for the next day, you will go into the night calmly, gratefully and happily and will sleep well and awaken gladly in the morning and accept the day as your good friend.

Through the exercises and through *actualization,* you will become a free, joyous child of God, who lives in great thoughts. If you live every day consciously and clear up what the day brings you, your spiritual consciousness will become more and more free and light-filled, from day to day. Through this, you will then be able to draw ever more profound wisdom from your expanded spiritual consciousness.

Guidance and support through the Inner Helper and Advisor in every situation – Example: oral or written test

Once you have become a person of the Spirit who lives his days conscientiously, that is, who lets his inner being grow to without by being alert and by actualizing, then you are more and more in communication with your inner being, the divine, the Inner Helper and Advisor.

Each day brings not only self-recognitions and experiences but also tests – including exams at school.

Someone who lives consciously and has followed his lessons at school conscientiously does not need to fear approaching exams. For your brain cells have absorbed what you need for the exam or the tests. The light-filled consciousness is in communication with the lessons stored in your brain cells. It becomes active when you ask the divine in you for help and support and absorb the exam questions consciously, which means concentratedly, looking at them conscientiously and reading them consciously word by word. You know: In every word there is the answer and the solution!

When, for example, you take a math exam, then be aware that in every number, too, lies the solution. Are you amazed? When you know that everything is vibration, that is, energy, then also numbers and mathematical formulas are energy, which radiates and communicates. In every energy is the positive part, the spiritual aspect, that knows everything, that also carries the answer and the solution to the math problems. If you have been attentive while the lesson was taught and if you have devoted your thoughts and your life to the divine in you, then the light-filled aspects of your consciousness will get in touch with the lesson in your brain cells and will communicate with the positive forces in the lesson and in the exam problem.

Now, when you have an exam question lying before you, then go briefly into the stillness, into prayer, just as I have already revealed to you, and ask the Spirit of God for support and help. Then look at the questions, read them conscientiously and entrust yourself to your Inner Friend, Helper and Advisor, the eternal Intelligence, and be alert, which means, trusting and concentrated. Suddenly thoughts can flow into you or sensations can awaken in you. Accept them, verify them with your intellect – and when you recognize the way toward the solution in them, or the solution itself, write it down.

Do not doubt in any situation! Because doubt locks the door to the light-filled consciousness – and a wrong answer can be the result. Know that the light-filled consciousness already knows every doubt of yours beforehand; it supports you according to your behavior. So strengthen your faith and your trust in every situation – and you will be even more sure of yourself.

When you have written down the solution, thank God, the Spirit of your heavenly Father in you, and be glad.

At the beginning of the Inner Path, you may try out what I have revealed to you. For this, God gives you the strength to increase your trust and your faith in Him, the eternal Intelligence.

After some time, when you have tried it and have grown strong, then what I have explained is applicable: The light-filled consciousness in you will react upon your doubts, fears and prejudices accordingly!

For oral tests the following also applies: The day before the exam, in the evening between 8 and 10 PM, when the vibrations of the atmosphere have calmed down and there is peace in the house or apartment, then go into the stillness, that is, into yourself, into your true being, and ask the Spirit of God in you for help on the day of the exam.

When through this you have become calm, pick up the material that will be tested. If you do not exactly know what the exam will be on, choose from your notes whatever you are urged to from within. Do not let your intellect alone lead you, but let yourself be guided from within! Do not reflect upon which page of the schoolbook you should open. Just open any page of your book. Trust that what you read will help you in the exam – even if it is only a rote definition upon which you can build.

During the oral as well as at the written exam, the same thing occurs: The rote definition can trigger a chain-reaction in your stored knowledge and result in the solution which you then express, orally or in writing.

It is written: Ask and you will receive! Ask Him, the great Spirit in you! And to thank Him, keep His eternal laws of love. Then you will also receive because you have prepared yourself for this.

When you go to sleep in the evening before the exam, consciously place yourself into the arms of the loving Father-Mother-God whose children we all are.

If you are still nervous externally despite the calmness in you, if your nervous system is excited, then you may take a natural remedy that strengthens your nerves, calms you, but does not make you sleepy. I repeat: a natural nerve-strengthening remedy that does not lull you to sleep – that is, it is not a sleeping pill; for a sleeping pill taken in the evening before the exam can have lingering aftereffects. Then it is possible that the next morning your brain cells are not fully active and cannot receive the impulses of the Inner Helper and Advisor, because the brain is still impaired by the sleeping pill.

So again and again, you recognize that the Inner Helper and Advisor, the light-filled consciousness, the Spirit of God in you, needs your brain cells that have stored the important lessons, in order to help the person, the consciousness.

You see how important it is not to burden your brain cells with unessential things, so they are stuffed with all kinds of things and you therefore can not consciously receive the divine in you. The Spirit of God needs a sounding board in order to communicate to you and to the environment. This sounding board is the stored data that you need for your life on earth. Even the words for this have to be present in the memory bank.

So if there is no memory bank in the brain, no programs, then nothing can flow. The whole person is controlled by the brain. So we could say: The person is the brain.

You have brought along programs of life into this world on earth. Take care that they do not become infiltrated by negative influences. Therefore, live consciously! This means: Whatever you do, do it completely!

Avoid all conversations that are merely idle chatter. If you have to be present at unimportant conversations, then participate only to the extent that you can bring out or contribute something that could be essential and of use for all participants. Your light-filled consciousness helps you with this.

The Inner Helper and Advisor is always present. Wherever you are, He is there, too.

A new day has begun. It is the day of your oral exam. You slept well – aware that God supports you. The first thought when awakening certainly concerns the exam. Nevertheless, thank our Father-Mother-God for the night and for the new day.

Despite your possible nervousness over what lies before you, do not let it upset you: Hold your short, silent devotion of the morning, in which you link with the Spirit, the light-filled consciousness in you.

Do not talk a lot on this morning and take only a light breakfast. Gather your strength and turn to your inner being; remain there! No matter what impressions want to distract you at home or on your way to school – stay calm.

If a schoolmate talks to you before the exam about his anxieties and fears, answer him in a calm and confident way; but do not let it trouble you. Perhaps – imperceptibly to you – your Inner Helper and Advisor can give a few hints, through you, to the anxious student so that he, too, will become calm and go into the exam with confidence.

When you sit in front of the board of examiners, turn your thoughts to within. Think briefly of the light-filled conscious-ness in you and affirm the helping divine power. When the exam questions are now asked, calmly take them in. Stay completely calm! While you take in the questions, the divine is already intensely active in you.

You have hardly taken in the questions and already the first thoughts rise up in you. Often it is only a short and seemingly unimportant introduction. But while you express the introduction, the light-filled consciousness in you finds its way to the stored data in your brain cells, which it needs in order to impart the solution to you.

This is how it continues: You have not yet finished the short introduction and you already know how to continue. Until you have spoken it, your Inner Helper and Advisor has already triggered further brain cells, to convey to you what should be added to the solution to complete it. All of this is *one* flow of thoughts without interruption.

If the examiner interrupts, do not let this irritate you. Often he is unconsciously stimulated by his light-filled consciousness to give you clues, which are impulses. These should activate those brain cells in you that your light-filled consciousness could not reach because you were, perhaps, slightly nervous and therefore, tense.

Know that anxiety is a lack of faith. It is not divine. Nevertheless, the Spirit of our loving Father, the light-filled consciousness in you, has great understanding for you, His child on this earth. He stands by you despite your anxieties. The Spirit of our beloved Father beholds your good will and rewards His child, who endeavors to live out of Him and to draw and give from Him.

Never forget to thank God for everything, also for the help with the exams – no matter how they turned out.

Do not doubt, and do not worry whether everything went well. Trust! God knows what is good for you: In everything, there is also the guidance for your life.

Your life on earth is predetermined in your soul as well as in your genes. During your life on earth, which you have created yourself through the light-filled and shadowed aspects of your previous incarnations, you can determine whether it takes a conscious or an unconscious course, which means, whether you increase your light-filled aspects or your shadowed aspects.

Someone who lets God guide him in every situation will not take any very long detours during his life on earth. He will be guided purposefully by the Father-Mother-God, from school age to a profession and to a professional life.

He will also be guided purposefully by the Father-Mother-God when choosing friends as well as when choosing a partner.

People who strive to live lawfully will also be guided when they enter into marriage or partnership, when they start a family and have children.

The one who gives honor to God and stays in communication with Him, the Inner Helper and Advisor, will not be misled. He will not go astray.

Programs – Predetermined aspects when choosing a profession – Inclinations and possibilities, memories and correspondences that are brought along

God, your heavenly Father, wants you to recognize yourself so that you can rise to any occasion.

You now already know that everything that moves you, every thought, every word and every sentence, every conversation, blow of fate, problem, illness, sorrow and need, joy and grief, contains the answers and the solutions.

You have also heard that many like-vibrating thoughts, words and actions combine and form a complex – we could also say: a program. Each complex radiates what it contains. It therefore expresses what vibrates in it.

Every statement, that means every vibration, already contains the right answer or solution. I call such linked-together thoughts, words and actions a complex or a *program.*

A person has created a lot of programs; many of them are stored in his soul and in his brain cells. Even your difficulties, problems, illnesses, needs, accidents and all blows of fate are various complexes that you once created through thoughts, words and your actions.

When the radiation of one or several constellations of planets comes into accord and thus, communicates with one or several of these complexes, that is, programs, which you have created, then these programs become active in your soul or in your brain. They then have an effect on your body – and you can fall ill or you get into difficulty with yourself or with some of your fellowmen. Problems and blows of fate can also be triggered this way.

Recognize: It is not your fellowmen who have inflicted these troubles and hardships upon you, but you have created them yourself! You are the hardship; you are the difficulty; you, yourself, are the problem; you are the fate; you are the illness.

God, our eternal Father, your Inner Helper and Advisor, wants to help you in time, out of everything you have created for yourself in time – before it breaks in over you.

He, the great Spirit, helps you to find the right answer and solution in all things. Every indisposition and illness, every joy and every sorrow want to tell you something. The positive parts of the complex, for example, of the illness, want to tell you how you should behave so that you can attain relief and healing through God and with the help of the doctor whom you may have consulted.

Ask God, your Inner Helper and Advisor, to help you in finding the cause or the causes that, for example, led to your illness. Entrust yourself to the Helper and Advisor in you; believe in Him – and you will receive the answer and solution.

Often it takes longer until you gain clarity concerning your situation. This can perhaps be because there are still human aspects, burdens, that lie over the divine part of your consciousness, so that your Inner Helper and Advisor can not reach you right away.

Nevertheless, He will not remain inactive, instead He will grant you help to remove these superimpositions of your human ego and to receive the answer and solution from Him. For this reason, be alert and accept those impulses that seem unimportant to you. Look at them, and whatever you recognize from them, clear it up!

The same applies for the positive aspects of your life. I have your choice of profession in mind here.

Already in the revelation for children from 6 to 12 years, I, Liobani, have spoken about choosing a profession. I would like to talk about it once again for you might not have read this revelation yet. Each of my revelations is complete in and of itself. If you have the possibility and read the previous revelations attentively, you will find there, too, explanations and understanding for your present situation.

Your Inner Helper and Advisor also helps you when you choose a profession! God knows His child! God looks into the light-filled as well as into the shadowed parts of your soul. He sees your genes, which carry your characteristics, which influence your life and shape "who or what you are."

Once you have gone through several lives on earth – and most souls in an earthly garment have done so – then you have already had several occupations, like, for instance, teacher, nurse, doctor, artisan, technician, employee, or you were a worker who acquired knowledge in several areas of expertise. The experience of such activities, namely, the ones you will need for your future lives, are registered in your soul as memories or correspondences.

Now, as your soul went to incarnation again, certain memories or correspondences became active because you need them as a human being, in order to help and serve your fellowman – or to come together in a profession with those with whom your soul created causes in previous lives.

What flows from your *memories* are already actualized aspects, which can be used to help selflessly and to serve your neighbor.

What flows from your *correspondences,* that is, what has been caused in a profession, is still a burden. It can be atoned for in a similar or the same occupation the person had practiced in a previous life: In his present occupation, he will be guided again to those people with whom he created the correspondences, the causes, within the professional sphere. At the same time, he receives the opportunity to make the best of the occupation, which at first was a correspondence, by carrying it out in a honest, straightforward and kind manner.

In your genes there can also be experiences of several elements of professions, which mean parts of the branches of professions that you practiced in former lives; they can become active at the right time insofar as you need them in this earthly existence. And then, when the time of outer maturity comes, when the young person reaches puberty and gradually enters adulthood, the occupational complexes of experiences, which are stored in the soul, become active.

If you are clear, that is, if you have opened up your divine consciousness partially or for the most part, because you lived consciously and cleared up what the energy of the days brought to you, then you will also receive help in choosing an occupation.

From the various activities of your former lives, several capabilities, talents and qualities can also rise in you. This can be expressed as follows: Once you want to become a doctor, and then you would like to be an artisan or a teacher. Or, in a girl, desires stir to become a seamstress, doctor or kindergarten teacher or to practice a social occupation.

When, during your schooldays, you have looked around in one or the other artisan or social area, which means that you worked there for a short time, to test your capabilities, talents and qualities, you will sense more clearly what attracts you and you will find more easily the occupation for which you bring along a larger potential of talents.

But if you find yourself at the end of your schooldays and only now think about choosing a profession that corresponds to your capabilities, talents and qualities, then consider the following: In every thought about the possibility to choose one or the other occupation, there is the answer and the solution.

When you like an occupation and consider whether to choose it for your life on earth, then again ask your Inner Helper and Advisor for assistance.

Because there are always various possibilities in you, your Inner Helper and Advisor, the divine consciousness, will not reflect into your feelings and tell you which occupation you should choose. But He will assist you in finding the occupation that fulfills you or in which you can clear up what you have caused in former lives, in the occupations of those times.

The Inner Helper and Advisor always strives to show you several possibilities that are active in you, and to guide you in such a way that your profession fulfills you and you can help and serve many people.

Yet it requires that it be possible for the Inner Helper and Advisor to guide you. Then He will show you aspects and possibilities from which you may recognize the significance of your various capabilities and talents. He will guide you, for example, to those branches of work for which you have an inherent greater potential.

The Inner Helper and Advisor can also guide you in this way: He shows you the possibilities within you through events, contacts, or insights – for example, during your holidays, on a walk or when visiting a doctor or being in a hospital. Or He guides you to people who tell about their occupational experiences so that you receive insight and can orient yourself accordingly.

When you are alert, that is, clear, you will feel more and more clearly which profession you should choose, and you suddenly gain inner certainty as to which is the right occupation for you.

Then you will either realize that you chose the right education for it – or you will change your classes or go back to school for a while or begin with an apprenticeship, depending on what you recognized. What you have learned and experienced until now, that is, what your divine consciousness was able to absorb and store for you, will be of use to you in your further life on earth.

Your parents' experiences with you can also be helpful. From the very first minute of your life on earth, they have accompanied you, looked after you and cared for you. Maybe they kept a book of insights on you where essential features of your childhood are written down. These enable you to look deeper into your thinking, feeling and living during your childhood. Your own journal, too, tells you a lot about yourself, provided that you kept it up conscientiously. In it you can find yourself and thus recognize your true being.

In the fast-moving time in which you are living, where events accumulate rapidly, you have certainly forgotten a lot in the meantime. The book of insights and your journal tell you what has been and what still is of importance. You can find yourself in them and also recognize whether your choice of occupation is good and is according to your capabilities, talents and qualities.

The spirit being in the earthly garment – To grow old and to wither – Find the truth, the "content of the capsule"!

Feel that you are a clothed spiritual being and a few years ago you slipped into a material cloak, the earthly garment. Think about this, again and again! You should shape and master your earthly existence in such a way that, after your human person passes away – when the cloak called human is taken off – you can return to the origin, to the light, where space and time do not exist.

Recognize that we are all children of eternity – regardless of whether you are in an earthly garment for a short time or I live as a spirit being in eternal existence. Space and time and day and night result from the condensation of spirit substance, called matter, which is no longer self-luminous – as well as from the movement of the globe, which rotates on its axis and revolves around the sun.

Man says: "It's the end of the day" when one part of the earth turns away from the sun because of the earth's own rotation. Or man says: "It's the end of a year" when the earth has revolved once around the sun. These movements of the earth are what man calls time.

When man has experienced a great many earth-revolutions around the sun, he is convinced that he has become old, because the years, as he calls the revolutions of the earth, determine his age. The fading of the earthly garment is determined by natural law.

The fine-material worlds, the spiritual stars know no shadows. They are radiated through and through, and therefore, shine from within. This means they are not *ir*radiated from without, like the material worlds are, but are radiated *through and through* by the Primordial Central Sun. It is the spiritual central star of infinity, which radiates throughout everything, so that all pure fine-material forms, as well as the fine-material worlds, shine of themselves. This is why, as you have already heard, there are no shadows and no night in the spiritual Being. It would be an error to think that day and night, space and time, would also exist in infinity.

The human body is subject to the changes of day and night. It feels good and youthful from within only when the person recognizes that his true being is cosmic. When he subsequently fulfills the laws of God, he will never grow old. His inner nature radiates youth through his withered skin. It is quite true that his physical body withers, since it is subject to the natural law on earth, for the body, matter, is viable only under certain conditions and only for a short time; but he will not age.

You must know that matter will one day dissolve – when all that is base, whatever is against the divine law, is transformed.

The base vibrations, the base ego, have once condensed to become matter; through the power of the central star, the Primordial Central Sun, and through the Redeemer-power of Christ, they will dissolve, that is, they will transform. Negative, unlawful energies will become highly-vibrating energetic, cosmic, fine-material power.

To be *old* means: to carry around old human thoughts with yourself and to let yourself be marked by them. To *wither* or *fade* means: The earthly garment, which is only a cloak of flesh and bone, withers and will one day be taken off. It is

131

possible that spirituality, the inner light, which the person has increased ever more on his path through life on earth, can shine through a withered skin.

A very burdened soul is still tied to the earth; it clings to external things and is therefore oriented to the world. After its physical death, such a soul will slip into a new earthly garment, a new cloak of flesh and bone, because by clinging to the earth and through its still existing causes, it is drawn back into this world.

However, once the soul has developed away from the ties of human thoughts, ideas and opinions, then it has awakened to inner youth and beauty – and the inner figure of light shines to without. Such a soul will not enter into flesh, but return to the Kingdom of God; the homeland for all beings, for you, too, is there.

So, *old* is only the person who has stood still in his spiritual development, who based his thinking and living on what is stored in his brain and believes that this is his life. You have heard that the brain should be a memory bank for whatever the spirit being in the earthly garment needs, not only for the things the person imagines.

To program the memory bank, the brain, solely with human data is human and not spiritual. Such people grow old and frail. The brain is also just as frail as the body: inflexible and forgetful. Such people can become childish in old age, because they live only in their past and talk about it. By doing this, they lose contact with reality, with the present life. Their bygone life is the present to them. They see it in the light of their conceptions.

Because they lack the inner values, the inner maturity, they exalt their external appearance and talk about their achievements, but – because they are constantly thinking about themselves – they mix everything up.

Because an "old" person recalls memories from the past over and over again and mixes them with the present, he no longer really knows, in the end, what is the past and what is the present. He exalts himself with everything, with his actions and with his suffering; or he talks about what he suffered or how good he was.

Recognize that to also speak about past suffering can be self-aggrandizement. Through this, the person wants to show off as a hero, who has come through this difficult past. Actually, he has not really overcome it yet. Because the one who talks about his past again and again, exalting himself or asking for pity, has not overcome it. In old age he lives in his past and has grown old, for his consciousness stayed back where his thoughts and daydreams are.

You now know the difference between growing old and withering or fading. People whose body withers can be young, even at an old age.

Their nature is cheerful and their spiritual consciousness is active. Their mind is awake and spirited. They react clearly in conversations and situations. The inner, eternal youth, the light-filled soul, shimmers through their age.

Such people radiate inner beauty and inner values despite being withered. The inner values are the inner powers; they flow from the divine law of love, peace and harmony. They bring about reason, understanding, tolerance and good will toward all fellowmen.

People of the Spirit radiate the inner values through their withering skin, through a spiritualized body. It served the soul as a mechanism, so that during the earthly years, that is, in the alternation of day and night, the divine consciousness could unfold. People who have unfolded their inner being are in communication with the Inner Helper and Advisor, the inner, eternal Intelligence, the giver of impulses, God.

When the soul has united with the cosmic consciousness, it has become divine again: the Absolute Law. It is again the spirit being of the heavens.

It is not your brain that is the intelligence in you, but the cosmic consciousness, your true self which is divine. A person's brain should serve the eternal Intelligence, God, as an instrument for this world. Your pure, flawless, light-filled consciousness is the divine in you. It is the Intelligence, God, the divine law.

The one who is able to draw from his true self is wise and intelligent. The brain of a truly wise person who is spiritually intelligent thus serves as an instrument, so that he can pass on what the giver of impulses, the Intelligence, God, the Inner Helper and Advisor, conveys to him.

But you must realize that words are merely symbols. Whatever infinity, the divine law, expresses in words via the brain lies *in* the word. It is the *content* of the word, not the word itself. Therefore the truly wise will not cling to the letters, but decode the symbols and words, and find the truth *in* the word, which is unlimited.

Someone who ties himself to the word, because he takes the word and the statement as such, as the criteria, is tied to the letter and blind to the truth. A comparison: He looks only at the capsule, the word, and seeks and therefore does not find the content of the capsule: the truth. The content of the capsule, the truth, is the lawful answer and solution.

If a person wants to know his neighbor as he really is, and not as he acts, he must first get to know himself. Someone who looks solely at the external appearance and takes the word as it is spoken knows neither himself nor his neighbor, because he is not able to look behind the words. Through this he is bound to the statement of the word, because he took merely the word and did not recognize its meaning. For this reason, he considers the word itself to be the truth. He looks only at the capsule, the word.

The content of the capsule can be explored only by the one who has explored himself. He recognizes his neighbor in his words and in his statements, because he knows himself. So the one who looks only at the capsule, the word, and has not explored the content is old in old age. Such people talk all their life solely about the capsule – their external existence – and do not know their true self. They have therefore wasted their earthly existence.

After physical death, this soul will again slip into a physical body, into a new capsule. And again, it will receive the possibility to find the content of the capsule – its true self.

Reincarnation is the slipping into a new capsule for the soul, which consists of all the former human aspects it has not yet discarded.

People who do not become aware of their true being, because they live past their life, will look only at their neighbor and value-judge and belittle him; one day, they will experience that their encapsulated ego will be broken open by the hammer called fate. The hammer, fate, consists of the manifested thoughts, words and deeds of the person. The hammer, fate, lets its weight fall upon the capsule, the ego. What then breaks open can be hardship, worry, illness, accidents or other things.

Fate can also guide two people together who have created a cause together and should now overcome it together. They are led together via indirect guidance, the constellation of the planets and the energy of the day.

Every time people are led together in the law of sowing and reaping, it is based on a binding between two or more people. The fact that two or more people are bound to a cause together can also be called the karma of fate: It has to be expiated by several people together, unless one or the other has disengaged from it in time, by living a life in the Spirit of God, by forgiving, asking for forgiveness and, if necessary, making amends.

A person who does not reflect upon his true being in time and strive to fulfill the divine laws will not escape from his fate, that is, from what he has once caused and is causing now.

And so, dear brother, dear sister, you not only have the chance to escape from your fate, which perhaps drew you into your human body, by actualizing in time, by forgiving and asking for forgiveness. By recognizing yourself in time, by actualizing and therefore dissolving the causes you have recognized, with what you have already overcome and kept within you as a mere memory, you will also be able to serve and help your neighbor who lives in his effects and has similar things to overcome as you once did yourself.

Recognize: Truly wise people help selflessly. The one who has conquered himself no longer thinks of himself.

A wise person has discarded his ego, his humanness, through actualization and looks into the true Being – as well as into the words of people and into the things that surround him. He also sees and hears what the one who merely looks at the word and listens for the word does not see or hear.

The wise man sees what cannot be seen. He hears what cannot be listened for; so, the word is merely a symbol: How a person speaks shows how he is.

Someone who cannot look into the words often gets a wrong picture of himself and of his neighbor. The *content* of the word gives the right picture of the person, not his word, itself. The one who sees a person as he is and not as he acts looks into the words of the person and sees in his word the person, as he is.

Every word is at the same time part of a picture. Several words together result in the picture. And so, the one who is able to look into the capsule, into the word and into the words, and at the same time listen into the words, sees the whole picture and hears from the picture what the person does not express.

What a person is like is also expressed in his external appearance: Shapes and colors of his clothes, his gestures, his facial expressions, his gesticulation, his hairdo and his shoes as well as his gait and movements show what and who he is. – The one who is able to see and hear in the right way will not go wrong.

Puberty – Storm and stress of senses and emotions – Love at first sight? – Don't suppress drives, but refine them – Outer or inner qualities of a man and a woman – Being in love or inner, selfless love as the basis for a partnership – Wrong kind of relationships – Mother or "clucking hen" – Significant settings of new courses during puberty

Dear sister, dear brother, you are now coming into or have already entered the age which is called the time of puberty. It is the development of sexual maturity.

Whether you are a girl or a boy, at this stage of development you are both impetuous and thoughtless. It is the time of storm and stress in your young lives.

A comparison to nature shall make these inner processes clearer: The development of the young person to an adult can be compared to the transition from spring to summer.

When summer takes its leave of spring, that means, when summer gradually comes, then spring storms still fight the mild summer breezes. But summer will succeed, because the sun rises higher and higher in the sky.

With adolescence it is quite similar: The young person gradually grows into adulthood. Even though all the features of a man or a woman seem fully developed in the young person, and he therefore feels grown-up and mature, he is still in a transition period from youth to adult. Yet he does not want to be considered or treated like a child or a teenager but as a grown-up.

Why is it exactly during puberty that the desire to be grown-up is so strong? The senses and emotions of the young person are still in storm and stress and only gradually find the way back into balance. This is done by the hormones which take over control only gradually.

You can compare the attuning of your world of feelings and of the senses with an antenna that has to be adjusted: Only when the antenna is adjusted precisely to a station, can the equipment receive the sound or the picture clearly. See, only when your hormones are in harmony with your feelings and senses, is your sexual life balanced as far as possible – to the extent the programs you have brought along allow it. You then are a man or a woman and are no longer in the process of growing or maturing into adulthood. You are physically mature, which means grown-up.

But now you are still growing. You are still in puberty and gradually developing into a woman or a man. During this time of storm and stress, you think you know everything better. You feel smarter than your schoolmates, your teachers, your parents and relatives. You feel exalted and look down on other people. You think they do not see things in the right light because they see them differently than you or because they do things in their lives differently than you imagine your life to be.

This leads you to judging and making value-judgments. One time you reject and another time you accept something, because you believe it is right, since it corresponds to your way of thinking and feeling. So, you think *your* standard is the only right one.

During this stage of development you are surprised that sensuality becomes quite intensely noticeable. It urges a boy toward the female and a girl toward the male. Both of them discover the other sex. A boy suddenly discovers the physical features of a woman on a girl and a girl discovers the attributes of a man on a boy. Sensual emotions are stirred, and girl and boy are attracted toward each other. A boy feels very comfortable in the presence of a certain girl and, vice versa, a girl in the presence of a certain boy.

Dear sister, dear brother, you will experience this for example at a school or a birthday party – whenever several boys and girls get together. You get along well with almost all of your schoolmates; but *one* girl or *one* boy gets your special attention.

What happened? Is this love at first sight? Examine yourself! Ask yourself *what* it is that you like about this boy or girl.

You have heard that nothing happens by chance, that everything is guidance. When a girl especially appeals to you, as a boy, then in you are either memories or correspondences.

You recognize the *correspondences* very quickly when you analyze your desires and thoughts and examine your *sub-communications,* which means, the sensations and feelings behind your thoughts or the symptoms of your body. Your body, too, which is in a stage of development, can become sexually aroused, which may perhaps draw you to a girl.

If it is only external aspects that attract you, then you can be sure that a correspondence is making itself felt in you. This could mean, for example, that you temporarily want to possess the girl's body – thus, these are sexual desires. It could also be the "fire of conquest": It is the urge of a man to conquer a woman for himself and to possess her in order to satisfy his desires. Or your desire is based on wanting to take a girl away from a rival, a former friend with whom you don't get along now. Or there could be simple carnal motives: You might, for instance, want to seduce a girl in order to test your sensuality.

All of these aspects you can classify in the law of correspondence – this means that you want something for yourself personally and for this, you want to use your neighbor.

In the girl the same aspects are not necessarily at work as they are in you. It is possible that this girl has similar correspondences as you do, but they could relate to another person, not to you. In this case, the girl will not respond to your desires at first.

However, if you keep sending your waves of thoughts and desires toward her, these can trigger correspondences in her, and finally, the girl may give in to your desires. In this way, you can both burden yourselves further, depending on what results from it.

The meeting with a similar vibration, that is, with the girl, made your correspondence well up. At first, this only wanted to tell you: You should clear up what you recognize, your correspondence, in time, *before* you meet the person who is tied to you by mutually created causes from one of your former lives.

The divine law always gives you the opportunity to recognize your desires – which are cravings that want to be satisfied through your neighbor – in time and to gradually overcome them.

When, for example, you realize that a girl does not respond to your correspondences – which means to your courting, which is your desire – then don't just drop her because you are disappointed. And do not speak disparagingly of her. The girl was just a mirror for you, in which you should have recognized yourself. By way of this girl, your Inner Helper and Advisor showed you what you should clear up – before perhaps one of your programs of fate hits you.

For a *blow of fate* is a complex of same or like vibrating sensations, thoughts, words and actions – a program you have created yourself.

So practice honesty and chivalry when a girl attracts your attention. Go to her. Talk to her and at the same time absorb her radiation. Ask your light-filled consciousness, the Inner Helper and Advisor in you, to let you absorb the positive radiation of this girl.

When the Inner Helper and Advisor is able to reach your brain cells, He will let you recognize via your senses – especially through your senses of sight and hearing – the inner values of the girl: You suddenly behold her gracefulness and hear words or sentences that impress you. Through this, you receive a completely different picture of the girl.

When your Inner Helper and Advisor, the light-filled consciousness, is able to guide you directly, then He will show you further lovable aspects on and in her that you will not want to destroy with your sensual desires. Suddenly, you feel attracted to the girl in a completely different way. The sensual thoughts turn into companionable thoughts and feelings – and now you see her as a person with whom you could perhaps develop a good friendship.

What happened? Your Inner Helper and Advisor showed you how to behave in a situation in which your body urges you to physical action, without there being a profound, uniting love.

However, when a girl responds to your physical acts of courtship and your body urges more and more, then ask yourself what you want to do now: Do you want to let your desires and cravings turn into a passion that keeps looking for new victims?

Or – to compare you to a young tree – do you want to ennoble yourself and prune the wild sprouts in time, before they get out of hand and drive you into a life of compulsion?

Or do you want to resemble an animal that has to be satisfied from time to time, but then also reproduces?

Or do you want to become a man? The characteristic of manliness is giving love. A man gives selflessly and also receives selflessly.

The decision is up to you!

Recognize, dear brother, dear sister: Puberty is again a decisive setting of direction for your life on earth. During this phase, you yourself determine the nature of your present and future earthly existence: Now you can still direct your senses more easily into a spiritual course, with your Inner Helper and Advisor, by setting the course for a noble life and thereby having an effect on your sexual desires and your world of senses.

Know that the senses of a person obey the one who obeys God. However, they play with a person who is a plaything for earthly and astral forces, for he does not take his life in hand but leaves it to seeming chance.

This does not mean that you should give up a sexual life. You should *ennoble* your sexual life in order to one day be able to accept and receive your wife or husband, to love him or her with all your heart.

Someone who has not learned to put order in his thoughts is also unable to curb his words or master his senses. Such a person is driven by his passions and thus, continually creates new suffering. This means that the one who does not have his earthly life under control, his way of feeling, thinking and wanting, his speaking and acting, is a hunted and driven person, who does not recognize himself and becomes a plaything for earthly and astral forces. He gives in to his passions and drives and is controlled by his correspondences. He becomes an instrument of earthly and astral forces that run riot through him.

I repeat: You should not repress your sensual feelings. That would be wrong. For anything repressed pushes to be discharged. The question is not to repress but to *refine*.

Every soul which has incarnated repeatedly brings along with it correspondences from its former human sex life again and again. For this reason, one is influenced more, the other less, by sexuality – according to the burdens brought along. Nevertheless, the Spirit of God gives every person the opportunity to ennoble these drives in time.

Often a young tree is refined before it bears fruit. Comparing this to you, it means: Before you become a man or a woman, you should ennoble your sexual life. In one's youth it is much easier than in adulthood. For in youth, one's sexual life has not yet been intensified by many years of activity.

If sexual desires are not stopped for a long time, they turn into passions. But passions can result in more passions: For example, gluttony, alcoholism, greed and much more. This holds true for boys as well as for girls.

A girl is also called upon to carefully figure out why her feelings and senses are drawn toward a boy – which thoughts and desires are behind it. A girl should also look for and find the inner values in a boy and take them into her inner being, into her light-filled consciousness. What the Inner Helper and Advisor then signals should be followed. Through this, the young tree is refined in time – and later the crown will not be overgrown with many thick side-shoots that deprive the tree of energy and do not let it bear the fruit that corresponds to its species.

To ennoble your senses means: Do not constantly preoccupy yourself with what your senses want. Sensuality shows itself in physical stimulation, in a man as well as in a woman. When a stimulated person now paints corresponding sexual pictures, he increases his sensual excitation and wants to experience his thought-pictures.

However, if someone who is sensually aroused paints a thought-picture that shows his partner surrounded by light and beauty, or as a pure vessel, which lets the partner be seen as a jewel or beautiful, fine china, then this picture will signal to him that he should behave accordingly. And so, he sees a child of God before him, in which the jewel, God, radiates. How shall he approach it? Passionately, with desire – or the way you treat fine, radiant china?

You hear and read again and again that the soul in a person is on earth to cleanse itself, so that it can again become a child of the heavens, a son or daughter of God.

The law of God says: A man shall let his virility flow during the physical union only when the man as well as the woman desire a child.

Virility will not flow when the man as well as the woman embrace each other in love and both do not work off the reactions of their bodies, but wish to unite in God. When both of them raise their sensations and thoughts to God, the sexual act will not be filled with pressure and compulsion. Then the physical union will be a mutual act of giving and not a mutual stimulation until the senses have reached their peak. Then neither of them desire the high-flight of sensual stimulation; they have the strength to let the physical union fade away in closeness and a happy union, without whipping up the senses.

This physical union is not unlawful; however, it is far from being the unity in God of all the cells of the body and all the particles of the soul. Only when this has been achieved, do both partners rest in God's love and give one another the selfless love from God.

When all the causes the soul brought along from former incarnations have been paid off, including sensuality, the pressure and compulsion for the human physical union will have been overcome. Man and woman will then come together physically only in a fine and noble radiation. This means the bodies will unite only when both wish for a child.

However, it is possible to fulfill this commandment of God only when the burdens of the soul concerning sexuality have been largely eliminated and the senses of the man and the woman rest in God and obey them – that is, when their thinking and living is aligned with God, the selfless love.

The still existing sexuality or sensuality should be ennobled to the effect that the man and the woman fulfill God's commandments. You have heard correctly: The selfless love between man and woman turns them into true lovers who trust each other, who can entrust everything to each other and are therefore open for each other. They have no secrets from each other.

When you, a young developing man, choose a girl to be your lady-love, then ask yourself what you recognize as being worthy of loving on the developing woman. Your senses can deceive you very quickly, especially when your nerves are craving relaxation. The same applies for a developing woman.

The girl should also examine whether the one who is courting her looks only at her external attractions or whether he looks deeper, at the inner values. The external attractions of a girl could be a smooth, youthful skin, a pretty face, an appealing figure or even wealth. With a man the external attractions could be good looks or a smart appearance, as well as his profession, his wealth and his car.

All of these and certainly many more aspects offer external comforts and attractions. In many cases, where these are striven for or are the basis for marriage, the partnership or marriage is built on sand. When it is not right from heart to heart, these external attractions and advantages will soon be secondary. They are still there, but lack a basis of under-standing, the ability to understand one another. The external pleasures are later taken for granted and one does not want to do without them; but, what good are all the external plea-sures when two people do not get along anymore?

In many cases, external pleasures are the sole bonds that keep a marriage or partnership together, because one wants to make his outer life as pleasant as possible. The life within, which alone turns an individual into a noble and fine person, can then no longer be developed.

The inner values pour from the inner, selfless love that does not expect anything – but gives itself.

The inner values of a man are steadfastness, faithfulness, trust, openness, solicitousness, straightforwardness. The man who truly loves is the protecting one, with whom the woman feels sheltered and safe.

Trust is an important part of the inner values. When a woman fully trusts her husband and a man fully trusts his wife, the man is neither jealous of his wife nor of another man. And the woman will not be jealous of her husband, nor of another woman. The woman trusts her husband and the man trusts his wife. Trust means: I trust her. I trust him.

The woman is sure of her husband's faithfulness and the man is sure of his wife's faithfulness. Out of this trust grows freedom, a with-one-another, and not a living next to each other or even leaning on each other. From a mutual openness, the man as well as the woman will act only virtuously. The woman, for example, trusts her husband when he leaves the house without her, when he goes to meetings, does business, is away on business or meets with friends or attends lectures in the evening. If possible, she will accompany him – and if she stays at home, she knows that she can be sure of him. Conversely, it is just the same.

The inner values of a women are openness, straight-forwardness, honesty, faithfulness, grace and beauty.

Beauty should not be mistaken for prettiness: Prettiness is a superficial "tinge" of a youthful body. Beauty is the radiation of the light-filled soul. It expresses itself, as already revealed, in grace, in harmonious movements of the body, in a well-balanced language, in harmonious gestures, in gentleness and understanding.

The inner values do not affect sexual drives. They radiate into the light-filled consciousness of the selfless loving person, who pays attention to the inner values.

After puberty, the inner values of a woman also include femininity. Femininity does not characterize the provocative or quarrelsome "wench." Neither does femininity represent a clucking mother hen that watches over only her own chicks, keeping only them in mind.

Dear sister, I would like to explain the difference between a woman and a "wench" to you:

A woman is self-possessed. She knows that her husband is a son of God and that she is a daughter of God.

A woman with unfolded inner values does not exhibit her external attractions. She dresses harmoniously but not provocatively. She does not drape herself with jewelry – but chooses a few discreet pieces. She is friendly, yet restrained and is a pleasant partner to her partner.

People who have inner values also radiate them. Whoever has an eye for them recognizes how they radiate from the overall appearance. The nature of such a person is pleasant. He does not want to be the focus of attention nor does he want to show off. He is just the way he is, himself.

A woman with inner values has a winning external appearance. The inner being is the aura of her appearance. She does not put on an act. This means that she is not emotional. Her nature and demeanor are harmony and the expression of inner beauty. A woman with inner values loves her husband; she is not in love.

Being in love often comes to an end very quickly. The ones who have fallen in love usually are in love with external features. If selfless love, the inner values, does not link them, these attractions soon will be exhausted and the external love becomes stale.

Just like it is with a woman, it is with a man. His inner values also bring about a pleasant, reserved appearance. His openness and straightforwardness radiate manliness and honesty, which he, however, does not use in sexuality but in his family as a husband and father, at his place of employment and in all spheres of his life where he voluntarily brings himself in.

The basis for trust is inner love. When a woman can trust her husband and vice versa, they develop a closeness and a love grows that unites them from within, that links them – but does not tie them. Selfless love is the bond of trust, of closeness.

Being in love is a flaring up of emotions that are triggered by external features. In many cases, being in love means to be tied or bound. A person who values only external appearances is also bound by them.

Attractions bind. They are something put on and artificial. They do not come from inner freedom, from God. Someone who falls in love with attractions, that is, with external values, soon becomes jealous. Jealousy is always intolerant and creates bindings. Being bound leads to being dependent, which results in quarrelling.

A partnership or marriage that consists of having once been in love and of habits, in which being closed and suspicion are the rule, shows various outgrowths. Once, the two had been in love with each other. But this state of being in love changed into an open or underhanded fight that is often carried out in arguments and acts of violence.

You can assume that whoever, be it woman or man, ties himself solely to external values, who falls in love with these, does not have them himself. He wants to adorn himself with his neighbor's external values. Actually, he wants to live through them by exalting himself with his partner's qualities.

The expression "You belong to me and I belong to you" says that the body of a partner also belongs to the one who fell in love with its physical characteristics and that he is allowed to make use of it. In this way, the woman often becomes a possession of the man and the man a possession of the woman.

This will to possess produces "wenchlike" characteristics in a man – just as it does in a woman: The "wench" leans on the man. She is nagging, jealous, quarrelsome, and anxious, because she thinks that her husband could deceive her or even leave her.

The "wench" expresses her claim to possession with words like: "You are my husband. Therefore, you have to fulfill these or those duties!"

She exerts pressure to make her neighbor, her husband, do what she considers to be right. She is jealous of her husband and of the female sex. She is constantly on the watch to see whether her husband is not indeed deceiving her. Through this, she deprives him of her trust. She is also of the opinion that he might have thoughts to which she has no access.

It is similar with a man as it is with a woman, resulting in effeminate characteristics in him. An effeminate man is a person of the male sex who leans on his partner or wife and, as a result, offers her no security. He is on the lookout for a female and tries to live through the external characteristics of the woman, to aggrandize himself through them.

The qualities of a woman that attract him could be: steadfastness that he does not have, security that he lacks, professional qualities that he did not acquire or wealth, to which he clings.

These and much more mark an effeminate man who often brings his wife into great difficulties – for by nature she is the receiving one and the effeminate man forces her into the role of being the giving one.

This is not in accordance with lawful giving and receiving. In this way, a woman can neither be nor become a woman – and the man cannot be a man, the giving principle, nor can he become a man.

Therefore, on earth, in your world, the harmony of powers should be restored between man and woman. A man should once again be the protecting, giving and guarding principle to which a woman can look full of trust. Then she knows herself to be sheltered, safe and secure.

A woman also has to become again the receiving, preserving principal who trusts her husband and feels sheltered and safe in his presence.

When the forces between man and woman are in accord, in harmony, then they love each other. Then they are not people in love with each other, who after being together for a short time fight each other, because each one wants to live his own ego through the other one, thus aggrandizing himself.

Dear brother, dear sister, so take care that you, the boy, become a man and you, the girl, become a woman – both with inner values.

Not every woman becomes a mother. Often there are deeper reasons for this. They can be purely spiritual reasons or be determined by the law of sowing and reaping.

A woman will become a mother when she herself has entered this into the cosmic law, either through her spiritual calling on earth or through the law of sowing and reaping. To have a spiritual calling means that the person has a spiritual task to fulfill on earth. This person can also burden herself. Then she will attract – according to the development of her soul – a light-filled or dark soul, exactly as she enters it into the law via her way of thinking and living.

You have already read about souls who are in the mission of God. Different spiritual criteria apply to these beings than to those who have left God, the eternal Intelligence, thus opposing Him, God, and are still doing so.

The soul of a person who created many causes in former lives will again attract those souls to which he or she is tied by former common faults.

Recognize that with every human, that is, every un-divine, thought, you are against God, against His eternal law, and you add to your own structure of fate within the law of sowing and reaping.

For example, someone who has sinned against an unborn child in a former life may not be able to have a baby in this life or she might receive just one child but not several. Or a child on whom the causes are already clearly visible is born into a family, which must carry the causes in a joint karma as an effect.

These are merely general hints. For you should know that the law of sowing and reaping, the causal law, consists of innumerable, interwoven karmic threads. You could compare it to a mighty, very fine-meshed net.

What is a good mother like, to which the expression *motherly* applies? She is the woman and mother who stays a wife to her husband and is a good mother to her children – who does not spoil them but cares for them. A good mother does not make children dependent on her, but brings them up to be independent and to have inner freedom.

There is also the mother who is a *clucking hen* because she constantly "clucks" over them. This means that she wants to push *her* experiences and ideas onto them and not allow them to be free. Her children accept what their mother considers to be good and right; therefore, they do not gather any experiences of their own. This may work well for some time. But then the children break out because, according to the eternal law, they want to be independent, free beings.

Such a mother cannot guide her children into the life. They do not experience the right way of life and a fraternal bond will not develop between her and her children. With this bond, I mean that father and mother should be friends and comrades to their children, but not dictators who raise their children in an authoritarian manner.

When a mother regards her child as her possession and forces her thoughts and habits upon it, this is not motherly but like a mother hen: She feeds her child with her own ideas and opinions, which she considers to be the only correct ones.

If the father is also like a mother hen, then neither of them will acknowledge the free-born being within their child. They want to completely keep it for themselves – which means the inner being as well as the external, the soul and the body – and want to forge the being, their child, as they consider to be right and good and not as the law of God wants it.

Recognize that with the procreation of a child, the father as well as the mother take great *responsibility* for the approaching soul and for the shell, the material body.

Someone who is aware of this will already grant the approaching soul respect and convey to the developing body, the embryo in the mother's womb, what soul and child need: good, harmonious, well-balanced thoughts and words and a corresponding behavior. These are forces that the developing embryo absorbs.

A person who lives his or her life conscientiously will wish the best for the developing child and for the newborn and will think and act accordingly. Therefore, one should think over his or her sexual desires. For a child is conceived quickly. If the child is then only partially accepted by its parents, the two of them create new causes.

When a woman has become a mother, she should, despite her motherly duties, remain the graceful, lovable, good-looking wife to her husband and not change into a clucking mother hen, thereby covering her inner beauty with her "maternal duties."

Dear sister, dear brother, during puberty you hold in your hands the decision as to how your further life will take its course. This is why I reveal that the years of puberty can essentially set a new course for this life on earth— and for further incarnations! If a soul does not incarnate anymore, then this life on earth also sets the course for the further development of the soul in the fine-material realms where it lives without a material body.

To the boy, the developing man, as well as to the girl, the developing woman, I now give hints about how they can shape their lives at this stage of their earthly existence, in order to be able to guide it onto a free and lawful course.

The *journal* still is of importance during puberty and can still give you information once you have grown out of puberty and have to prove yourself in your occupation and start a family. If your parents have already kept a book of insights for you, their child, and have carefully noted the pros and cons of your behavior – and also their reactions toward you, the timid or angry child – then you can gather much from it about what now happens during puberty. For example, sexual outbreaks or strong aggressions of a young person can have their causes in childhood.

If a child was forbidden more than given suggestions during its childhood, it may have repressed many things, out of fear that its parents would scold or even spank it. Such repressed fears can take effect precisely during puberty as a sexual impetus or aggressions.

From a book of insights, one perhaps can see why a teenager now behaves the way he or she does. It is also possible that the parents, from what was written in the book and the problems of their child during puberty, recognize their own wrong behavior. If the parents can now talk about this with the teenager, then, by asking for forgiveness and by understanding, many a thing that troubles the teenager during puberty could be overcome.

If there is no book of insights, it would be good if you, dear brother, and you, dear sister, would note everything into your journal that strongly moves you or that triggers aggressions or depressions in you. In the journal you can note every day what especially moved you or caught your attention.

When you have the same or similar problems over and over again, that is, when the same or similar thoughts, aggressions, depressions or fears come up, ask yourself what triggered these ill-feelings: which thoughts you had shortly before or which occurrences led to it. Note your insights in your journal – if possible, including date and time.

You have already heard that when, for example, aggressions or depressions occur or when states of anxiety afflict you or when strong sexual desires come up in you, then several things must have taken place in your thoughts or through your senses. This means that you carry the various correspondences in you that call up these emotional turmoils in you. When your thoughts – while you do something or while you look at certain objects – come close to the same or similar thought complexes, then the correspondences in you start to communicate with the thought complexes around you or in the atmosphere. These cause the states of anxiety, the depressions, aggressions or intense sexual desires in you.

Also certain physical movements, an object that reminds you of certain events, or also people or pictures can trigger these energy fields. Through this, a flow of energy develops – I also call it communication – which the correspondences in you stir up more strongly, as I have just described.

If you have noted such recurring conditions or circumstances in your journal, including date and time, then it will be easier to reconstruct what brings about such conditions.

You know that in everything lies the answer and the solution! Once you have recognized what triggered these symptoms, you can also find the corresponding answer and solution.

When you have recognized the root of your human outbursts and cleared it up, note this, too, in your journal. Write down, for example, how you conquered your aggressions or depressions, that is, how you became free of them and what the results of this were for you.

The positive as well as the negative aspects in your journal serve you for further self-recognition – and also for the strengthening and maturing of your inner being. When you find yourself in a similar situation again one day, then your journal will help you. Your journal is a good companion to you: No matter what situations arise, you can always look up your notes.

Your journal will also give you impulses by which you can establish communication with your Inner Helper and Advisor. Often the intellect cuts capers and for this reason, the person no longer has access to his inner being. The notes in your journal can then guide you to the Helper and Advisor in you again. When you read it attentively and feel glad about what you have already overcome, about what has already become divine in you, you become calmer and more secure and can face a new situation serenely. In this calm you gain contact again with the Inner Helper and Advisor who always wants to support you.

Never turn away from your parents. Aim to be good friends and companions with them! Nurture openness in every situation. Then you can talk about everything, about joy and about problems – and your parents will do so, as well. This connects you and gives you strength for a common, comradely life on earth.

Dear brother, dear sister, gradually the time of puberty draws to an end. Your emotions become more stable, because you have now overcome the time of storm and stress, for the most part. Every now and then it may still show up a bit. But you know when spring turns into summer, cool rains can still fall, even though the fields and woods are already green.

Have you graduated from school yet? Are you still studying? Or do you already have a good start in a profession? – The Inner Helper and Advisor guides each one according to his abilities, talents and qualities. Every lawful profession is important for the well-being of many people.

Your professional life – Attitude toward work and income – There are no coincidences, also at work – Colleagues and the law of correspondence – Polarity – The philosopher's stone – Become impersonal and wise!

Your profession can also be a *vocation* – if you let yourself be guided by the Inner Helper and Advisor. He does not take any detours with you. He knows you, His child, and knows what you need as a human being. He also knows which profession you should choose that matches your aptitudes and in which you could be happy.

The Spirit of God in you, the eternal Intelligence, strives to guide you directly. He can do this when you heed the impulses of the day, when you live the day consciously and stay in communication with the divine in you.

If, however, you hold yourself up with your own problems and difficulties or if you are preoccupied with things that do not relate to you, for example, the behavior of your fellowman, and you ask yourself how he might think or talk about you – then you turn away from the Inner Helper and Advisor. Such human behavior distracts you and turns you into a slave of your own ego. You keep thinking about the same thing and therefore cannot perceive the impulses from the divine in you anymore.

Someone who cannot concentrate on *one* thing, who ponders over things and occasions for days without clearing them up, may perhaps take many detours – until he finally ends where his task lies, the place where he can work the most effectively according to his spiritual task or according to his abilities, talents and qualities.

You know it now: God can guide you directly if you actualize His commandments and let yourself be guided. They are excerpts from the eternal, cosmic law of the heavens.

Only the actualization of the commandments gives your life a lawful orientation. It is only then that God can, for the most part, guide you directly, through the Spirit of love.

When it is possible for God to guide you directly, then your profession can also be a vocation. At your place of work, where you are, you can go to work accordingly and prove yourself. Perhaps you can also clear up something left there from a former incarnation – either with a certain colleague or you can finish a certain task which you began in a former life. At the same time, you can help and serve many people by way of your profession and thus, contribute to the common good in the world.

When you have chosen your profession, then act just like in school: Do your job conscientiously!

The work that the day brings you, too, can tell you a lot and bring you joy. Be conscious and focused in what you do. Whatever you do, do it selflessly. Then you are serving your neighbor selflessly. Be aware that people who act selflessly show inner greatness.

This does not mean that you should not be paid for your work. Just payment is due to a just worker.

Yet when you render services after your regular working hours, that is to say, when you work overtime, then do not think: How much will I earn for this extra work? You have a fixed salary and will certainly be paid more for your extra work. But do not constantly think about how much money you will earn from this. Make it a habit to give – without asking what you will receive in exchange. Constantly thinking about money and goods constricts your consciousness and makes you petty and narrow-minded.

Strive to be selflessly active at all times, without expecting recognition – even if you know that you will receive money and goods. Do not think only about the payment while you work. Work selflessly without asking whether the one has more to do than the other.

When you fulfill your duties in this way, you will become rich within. The one who has become rich within will also possess everything he needs externally, and beyond that. Try it!

When you accept work after your working hours, during your free time, in order to help your friends, neighbors or the community you belong to – whether it be in the house or on the fields or anywhere else – do not immediately think of recognition and payment.

Strive to do every job conscientiously. Then you will soon recognize that through your neighbor, God has rewarded you many times over. Every selfless service is a divine service and is rewarded by God. But do not say: "I expect God to reward me." Do not expect anything – trust! God has not forgotten you.

This does not mean that you should not learn a profession or that you should work only when an opportunity offers itself! Learn a profession and comply with the working hours. For this, you will be paid by your employer.

Do not think less of your colleagues' work than of yours and do not belittle them and their work. Each person has different abilities and each one is of a different nature, according to his spiritual maturity. Every person fulfills his work from his inner or outer attitude. Do not look at your neighbor. Just look at yourself and work on yourself, so that you can understand your fellowman.

A wise person does not judge. He sees and knows. Only the spiritually blind person judges, because he neither sees nor knows himself.

Recognize: Someone who gives his neighbor freedom of thought and living and does not lecture him will create a good and friendly atmosphere at work with his colleagues, where one can work well. You have to always be aware of the fact that every person should develop freely.

You can share your opinion. You can also explain, if, perhaps, disagreements arise or if things do not go as it would be good for all concerned. But you should not force your will and your opinion upon any person.

There are enough know-it-alls in this world. And particularly the know-it-alls have contributed to the fact that this materialistic world cannot last. It will pass away and with it, the know-it-alls.

After this turn of time, the new world in Christ will open. So, step by step, you are entering a New Era. For this reason, prepare yourself for it!

The world of Christ will not be governed by know-it-alls but by the Spirit of the Lord – and all people are brothers and sisters in Christ. The coming generations of people will follow the divine laws more and more and have *one* leader: Christ.

The Kingdom of Peace of Jesus Christ will develop on this earth. Just as the eternal, divine order exists in the eternal Kingdom of God, so will the divine order open up in the Kingdom of God on earth. Until this New Era, until the Lord of Life takes up the rulership of the purified, new earth, *The*

Regulations for the Community are valid for the developing Kingdom of God on earth. If you have not yet heard about this, then get the Christian regulations for the community. It is called: "The Shepherd and His Flock." There, you can look up many of the things that are already familiar to you from this revelation, for example, how you should, already now, conduct yourself at your place of work and in the world.

Recognize that there are no coincidences! It is not by chance either that you work with these and not other colleagues or that exactly this person is your boss. It is also not a coincidence that you work in this and not in another firm or in a different branch office. Coincidences do not exist!

You will very soon notice that with some colleagues you have a trusting relationship at work, while with others, you feel a certain distance. What is the reason for this? It is quite similar to the situation with your former teachers, schoolmates and friends: There is something you cannot quite figure out. Yet you sense it when you meet certain colleagues, or when you talk with them. Even though there has never been an unkind word spoken between you and your fellow workers, even though you are friendly when you meet and work together, from time to time something vibrates that does not let you come together from within. What is it?

There are forces – we also call them correspondences – which may have brought you together, but do not let you find your way to each other. With correspondences, I mean the contrary, human aspects, which we also call karma. Karma is a guilt of the soul.

So karma is what led you together. Like attracts like. The unlawful attracts, in turn, unlawfulness, like or equally vibrating karmic forces.

The positive, the lawful, attracts positive forces, thus, people who vibrate identically in positive aspects. They immediately hit it off with each other, go toward one another and make friends.

People who should clear something up with each other may perhaps also go toward the other, but they cannot warm up to each other. If this is how it is with you, or something like it, then karma, the correspondence, wants to get your attention with a "long arm," for you to analyze the so-called antipathy which you feel: Ask yourself what you don't like about your neighbor, what you might be jealous of. Or ask yourself what you disapprove of or what upsets you about him which you perhaps use to belittle your colleague.

Seek and find the answer and solution in yourself: What is the basis of it in you? If you are jealous, then ask yourself: why? Why do you disapprove of the thoughts and actions of your neighbor? Why do you get upset about him? Or, when your neighbor says or does something or other, what or how do you think about it?

Such and similar processes should stimulate you to think it over. Your neighbor is merely a *mirror* for you. Find in yourself whatever it is you find wrong with him – and therefore, with yourself, too. For whatever upsets you about your neighbor, you have the same or like aspects in yourself.

Ask the Inner Helper and Advisor for support so you can recognize in and on yourself what you should clear up. Not your neighbor, your colleague, has to clear up what concerns you, but you alone! What your colleague has to clear up concerns only God and His child, that is, God and your neighbor – not you. So, examine yourself!

Never forget that every person has many good qualities, even though it often does not seem to be so, because the person has covered over the internal treasure, the cosmic jewel, his true self, with many human thoughts, desires and longings, with hatred and enmity. Despite all this, the good is there. For without this power and the source of this power, man cannot live.

Someone who is able to see through the filth of the human ego will find the *"philosopher's stone,"* the love, the strength, the divine.

God Himself, the Eternal, gave Himself to His children and made them the heirs to infinity. The heritage of each spirit being is the eternal law, God, the gem, the life in God.

Everything is consciousness. Pure being is purest consciousness; it is divine. This is the heritage from God.

God is God from eternity to eternity. He is the Father and Mother of all His children. The power of the Father-Mother-God, the inheritance, the life, the eternal law, is effective in all spirit beings – this signifies equality of all His children: All spirit beings, no matter whether they are positive or negative principles, that is, man or woman, are divine and are on an equal footing and are bearers of the divine law.

In the *male principle,* the male, that is, the "positive," natures and attributes are active. They are the giving and protecting powers. They are called the "positive," the male, energies.

In the *female principle,* the receiving and maintaining powers are more active. They are called the "negative," the female, energies.

In the eternal law of God, the positive and negative powers are the energies of the natures and attributes. The spiritual powers, positive and negative, have nothing to do with the human, moral terms of "good," "worse" or even "bad," as they are used to value-judge in the law of sowing and reaping. They are spiritual-divine polarities that complement one another so that the forces may flow.

The divine powers – the positive and the negative poles, respectively – are giving and receiving in constant interaction with each other. From this, flows all life for the spirit beings, souls, humans, minerals, plants, animals and stars. The whole of creation is based on polarity, on giving and receiving, the positive and the negative principles.

Through these two poles – giving and receiving – the eternal Spirit breathes. He respirates eternity, causing more and more light and power to flow into infinity. Out of the giving and receiving life, further spiritual forms of life develop in the heavenly worlds: the spiritual minerals, the spiritual plant and animal kingdoms, the nature beings and the spirit beings.

Thus, the life from God is also in every human being. It is the divine consciousness that bears within all spheres of life as essence. This is the gemstone in man, the eternal law, God. This gemstone is also called the *philosopher's stone.*

The one who has fully opened the philosopher's stone, the divine consciousness, as a human being, lives in the law of God for the most part and, even as a human being, personifies the law of infinity in word and deed. And so, you will find the philosopher's stone only when you gradually fulfill the laws of God, that is, when you live them in your everyday life. Only by fulfilling the eternal laws, that is, by living according to them in your daily life, will you find the philosopher's stone in you: It is your light-filled consciousness, the divine in you – the Inner Helper and Advisor.

Neither by talking about the laws of God nor by looking at your sins and faults, will you find the philosopher's stone in you and become wise, but solely by repenting of your sins and faults, by discarding them and no longer doing them. Then you will gradually fulfill God's will and become wise.

Practice affirming the philosopher's stone, the divine consciousness, in your neighbor, as well. There are many terms for the philosopher's stone: You can call it the divine power and might in all Being and in mankind; you can also designate it as the divine consciousness or the eternal truth or the law – or the gemstone or the wisdom of God or the Absolute.

Recognize that the words themselves are not wisdom, but what is in or behind the words. Here, in the depths, the wisdom, the philosopher's stone, can be beheld and hearkened. Therefore, learn to hear your neighbor's words not only as such, but learn to listen into the words.

Once you no longer judge your fellowmen, or condemn them or talk unlawfully about them, you can hear from their words what was not spoken.

A wise person receives the light, the wisdom, from the gemstone and will – when necessary – address impersonally what he has recognized. This can happen via a question or a counter-question or by a lawful answer. Impersonal questions or answers are selfless.

And so, recognize that a wise person will not address the truth directly, especially not when talking to people who are still living and struggling under the law of sowing and reaping, and are only gradually attaining the law of inner freedom. Although a wise person recognizes what it really is about, he may not address directly what he has recognized. Via questions and counter-questions, he must *guide* the person to his own recognition.

You see, according to the divine law, a wise person may not directly tell his neighbor the truth, which he heard and perceived in his neighbor's words. As long as his fellowmen do not live in the divine consciousness themselves and do not act in the law of God, but are still in the law of cause and effect, a wise person will guide his neighbor to recognition via questions and counter-questions. Through this, deeper layers of his neighbor's consciousness are nudged, which, until then, he was not aware of. They then start to vibrate. Their contents, or parts of them, will arrive in the consciousness of the person either immediately or in due time. Then, he will realize that the wise person, maybe quite some time ago, told him from the truth, which he, the person, can understand only now.

And so, a wise person addresses his fellowman impersonally, but only when it is necessary and when the latter wants to gain recognition about himself. In so doing, a wise person remains fully calm, which means that he rests in himself. His inner calmness, even while explaining about unlawful matters, indicates the impersonal life in the wise person. He is not biased and not emotional.

Recognize from this for yourself that when you meet your colleagues from within, out of the divine love and wisdom, you can express and address many things. It will flow from your inner being and be mostly impersonal. However your neighbor reacts – it will not affect you, because you did not speak from your ego.

So, when you find the good in your fellowman and keep it in you, you will always have access to the inner being of your neighbor. Only on this basis of inner understanding, is it possible to live on this earth fearlessly, tolerantly and without pangs of conscience. A person who is just toward himself and toward his neighbor does not need to have a bad conscience toward his fellowman because of his behavior.

Once you have conquered yourself to the extent that you no longer judge and condemn your neighbor, the day will approach you differently – in a light and bright way.

It will then show you again and again what you have already overcome. It brings you joy and peace. At the same time, it shows you which level of purification you are still on – and what you should overcome today.

With an example, I want to make clear to you how the day and your Inner Helper and Advisor can guide you: Let us assume you meet a good-looking person. His appearance is attractive and well-groomed. This person fascinates you. Your eyes rest on him and you feel agreeably touched. What is it that you like about this person?

The person who is growing wise, whom I consider you to be, goes to the Inner Helper and Advisor and asks what fascinates him so much about this person. If your consciousness is developed to the extent that the Inner Helper and Advisor can answer you, drops of life rise up out of the deep ocean of love. Some of these drops of the Spirit then stimulate some of your brain cells – and you sense what it is that so fascinates you about this person! Is it the way he moves? Is it his well-groomed clothing or its harmonious colors? Or is it his radiation, which is expressed in his movements and his clothing?

The day and the Inner Helper and Advisor want to tell you, for example, when you saw your neighbor, that your inner being and your external appearance are also in accord with each other and that you vibrate in a way similar to this person, that the same or like aspects are thus in and on you.

Be happy about this, for in this way you are shown that you, too, have already overcome some things in your life, for you were agreeably touched and enjoyed your neighbor's radiation.

Such and similar occurrences are brought and shown to you by the day and the Inner Helper and Advisor. Through this, you can recognize fairly well which spiritual level of life you are on: Whether you can enjoy your neighbor's radiation because the same or like aspects are in you – or whether you still judge, assess and compare.

Even stars, oceans, lakes and rivers, trees, grasses and animals trigger the pros and cons in people: the selfless and calm, as well as the emotional and destructive. Only when a person has spiritually matured, will he feel in himself that he is in communication with all life forms and is linked with them in God's unity. He will meet God in all life forms and his Inner Helper and Advisor will be active and he will be constantly aware of Him.

Whoever has found his way to his Inner Helper and Advisor, God, is largely united with Him via the soul. He has entered his divine heritage and begins to draw and speak from the treasure of the wise – from God, from life. Then the days will become brighter and friendlier for this person. And so, it is worthwhile to become wise!

Wisdom has nothing to do with knowledge. You can have the knowledge from all the books of this world and still not be wise! You can find the philosopher's stone, the divine within the person, your true self, only by striving to *live* according to the divine laws.

It is worth the effort. Overcome your ego, even if it means great effort!

Once you have overcome yourself, you are wise.

Wise people are *level-headed.* They do not rush into things by making rash decisions. This also applies at work.

Do not strive with the means at your disposal for a position in your occupation that seems agreeable to you, and do not climb the rungs to a better and higher position by force. You may very well aim at achieving this or that – and if it is God's will, it will happen. But do not force it by unfair means and methods. Stay righteous in word and deed.

Do not force anything in your life. Be aware that justice will be done to the righteous and the honest. God guides you!

If you are meant to receive a prestigious position in your occupation, your Inner Helper and Advisor will direct everything accordingly.

No matter what job you are charged with, strive to carry it out conscientiously and honestly.

Dear sister, dear brother, you have now received a lot of help from the Spirit of love. Over and over again, I explained the same and like things to you from various facets of divine wisdom. Therefore, take in these repetitions, too!

Know that all this help and all this advice come from the divine wisdom. When you accept this help and advice and do what you have been advised, you will become wise.

A truly wise person keeps the laws of the earth insofar as they are in accordance with the spiritual laws. You are a citizen of this world, but equipped with gifts of the Spirit. For this reason, you will wisely weigh with the power of the Spirit what is to be done, in order to keep the laws of this world and respect the laws of God.

When you are on your way to becoming wise – which means to develop the wisdom of God in you – then you will become one who beholds and hearkens. This means that you can see through a person and behold what he is – not how he acts. You hear what he does not express, what vibrates in the unspoken word, namely, what resounds in the spoken word, that is, what sounds behind the word.

Whoever looks will see only the external appearance. The person who *beholds* will behold in the depths, in what cannot be expressed.

Whoever listens will hear only the word. Someone who *hearkens* will hear into the word.

A person who has learned to behold and to hearken will no longer condemn or judge other people. He knows them.

A true wise man cannot be deceived, because he has learned to behold and to hearken. For this reason, he does not set great store by what his neighbor pretends, the external appearance, the external speech, the external gestures.

A wise person is quiet: He beholds and hearkens into his fellowmen and into their words.

People who spiritually grow and mature do not increase their still existing burdens: They are constantly alert, to see that they conquer their still remaining human aspects and to no longer live the correspondences that they have recognized, so that these will not multiply through this. Someone who grows spiritually is alert and does not let his correspondences dominate him.

Dear brother, dear sister, when your eye catches sight of something external, when it sees something, then turn within and learn to behold! When your ears still want to listen for something then turn within and learn to hearken!

If you are alert during your life on earth, you will recognize in time the correspondences that still exist in you and, with

Christ, transform what perhaps could lead to problems or even blows of fate.

Someone who has learned to surrender himself trustingly to the Inner Helper and Advisor, the Spirit of God, will be guided and advised lawfully in all questions of life. This applies to every situation – at work as well as in all other activities – no matter what comes to you. It applies just the same when choosing a life companion.

Someone who knows his inner values will also recognize the inner values of his neighbor.

Choosing a life companion – Criteria: outer or inner values – Tasks when living together – What attracts you? What do you strive for?

I, Liobani, will now shed light on the choice of a life companion from another facet of the truth.

Meanwhile, you have learned not to simply look at the external appearance – whether a woman is pretty or whether the man has a good position at work and knows how to behave well in society – you look deeper!

When you now have gained maturity and the desire for a life companion awakens in you, then ask your Inner Helper and Advisor about it.

During puberty you surely went through some experiences with the other sex. Nevertheless, it is possible that with the desire for a life companion you are first led to a person with whom you still have to clear up something according to the law of sowing and reaping.

Let us assume that you meet a young person who looks good to you and to whom you feel attracted: Ask yourself *what* attracts you!

I, Liobani, have already given you several criteria that show you whether there are correspondences attracting you, that is, karma – or whether it is the person's inner values that link with your inner values. Apart from that, you have the Inner Helper and Advisor, who, according to the law of free will, will support you in reaching a free decision.

If you do not want your karma to be reinforced or even grow bigger, then pay attention to the following advice: When karmic bonds become evident, you do not necessarily need to dissolve them in such a close relationship as a couple. This is only unavoidable when there is something very serious, a binding soul guilt, which can be dissolved only in this way, that is, in a marriage or partnership.

Many other karmic threads can be dissolved in a marriage or partnership that is based on the inner values or on a good, open friendship. Therefore, examine yourself! Examine your feelings, your thoughts and your senses!

External signs that might point to karmic threads are the following:

If the chosen one shows off his external appearance, that is, places it in the foreground, if he offers his attractions and attributes, these are most likely traps. Take notice of the clothes. How is the clothing of the person you would like to choose: clean or dirty? Are the colors of his clothes glaring or disharmonious – or are they soft colors that are coordinated with each other? Shoes can also tell a lot, as well as the way a person moves and walks. His speech, his eating and drinking habits, punctuality or unpunctuality also show who he is. Only an unknowing person looks at the external appearance and lets himself be deceived by it.

A wise person sees, beholds and recognizes what the one who parades before the wise person does not know, himself.

One criterion for living together well is *sense of duty*. A sense of duty, regarded from the point of view of the Spirit of God, means: All the tasks that a person undertakes should be fulfilled conscientiously and faithfully – toward people and the matter at hand.

People who live in a marriage and partnership should also have a sense of duty. The man as well as the woman has duties in a marriage and partnership. When they fulfill them out of a sense of duty, they become gifts of love stemming from selflessness.

All duties and activities are a part of selflessness when they are conscientiously carried out with the Inner Helper and Advisor. It is the man's duty of love to care for the woman, to protect her and to keep her in his heart.

When a man has taken a woman into his heart and vice versa, a woman has taken a man into her heart, then faithfulness is also guaranteed. A person who is faithful with his senses is also faithful in his thoughts, words and actions. Out of faithfulness grows inner love, if the man as well as the woman meet each other in selfless love.

The man also has a duty of love to care for his children. Father and mother should strive for their children to become honest, kind and conscientious people whom one can rely on. And the woman and mother has the task to maintain the family and to make life in the family friendly and pleasant. The duties of love of the woman are to safeguard the gifts which the man brings and to tend to what keeps the family together. She is also the *keeper of the hearth,* but not the little housewife at the stove.

The "keeper of the hearth" means that she watches over the communal life in the family and endeavors to see the arrangement of the apartment or house as her job, so that her husband and children feel well there. Thus, she is not the "little housewife" who only cooks, cleans, does the laundry and looks after the children.

Above all, she is a wife and mother; however, beyond the family, she can also carry out professional duties part-time, or an activity that corresponds to her mentality and her present level of consciousness.

In the communities of the Lord, there are living communities and father-mother-houses; therefore, the woman does not have to stay at home all the time.

The members of the *living community* take turns with the communal duties. Thereby, each one has to fulfill his duties in the living community at a certain time. By alternating communal duties, free hours become available to the members.

The *father-mother-houses* are large living communities for children where one or two foster mothers take loving care of the children so they do not lack anything.

If you want to know more about this, then read the regulations for the Kingdom of Peace of Jesus Christ "The Shepherd and His Flock," as well as "Liobani. I Tell a Story – Will You Listen?" and "Liobani. I Advise – Will You Accept?"

Dear brother, dear sister, you now have something to go on in choosing a life companion who corresponds to your inner values.

You have heard that like forces attract each other. Now it is up to you which forces you activate in yourself. These forces will then serve as a magnet for a partner. They will attract either inner values, the spiritual forces, or simply external ones.

When your active inner values come in communication with those of your neighbor, then you will establish a *union*. But if you activate only your external characteristics, the energies or stimulations of the senses, they will combine with the external attributes of your partner and *bind* you to them.

So, it depends on your attitude and on the level of development of your spiritual consciousness, as to which partner you attract.

The good – whatever is good and lasting for a life on earth – comes from within.

Whatever is striven for solely externally can also seem to be good; but it can soon break apart – or it can result in a mutual toleration, a living next to each other, but not with each other. Coming together externally can happen through amenities and comforts, but it can become quite agonizing after a while – namely, when the two people have nothing to say to each other anymore and merely live next to each other. External criteria lead to ties. Whereas, selfless love, a togetherness, a union can grow from the inner values. Where there is a union there is also spiritual growth. Where bindings prevail, there is stagnation and difficulties arise.

Marriage or partnership: a covenant with God – Document of vows between the two life companions – The spiritual-ethical principles for a good marriage or a good partnership – Harmony within and externally

You have chosen your life companion. If you wish to form a covenant with God for your life on earth, then both of you should turn within. Go before the Spirit of God in the sanctum of your inner being and ask Him to bless your path through life on earth.

God, our Heavenly Father, looks into the hearts of all people. Before Him, it is not important whether you seal a marriage at the registry office or choose a partnership, that is, a union between the two of you and God without going to the registry office.

Before God, both marriage and partnership are a union. Whoever asks God for His blessing forms this union before God; he enters a *covenant* with God for his earthly life. To ask God for blessing and guidance is a covenant with God. The bond between the two who love each other then links them with God. The one who asks God for His blessing has given his neighbor a vow of faithfulness and love. Faithfulness and love to God is also faithfulness and love to one's life companion.

It is a sanctified step into a joint life when the community of the two partners is formed in the sanctum of the inner being, before God, the Almighty. The woman as well as the man should be well aware of this.

The one who asks God will receive. God gives and will always stand by those people who ask Him to and who keep His commandments.

Someone who violates the commandments again and again, also in marriage and partnership, breaks the covenant with God. A person who dissolves his marriage or partnership for purely material or sexual reasons rejects God's help.

This does not mean that a separation in marriage or partnership is against the eternal law in all cases. An external separation can take place when one of the two partners strives for higher ideals and values, while the other wants to live out his desires in the world. However, this should be carried out only when the one who prefers the world is disturbed by the decision of the other one and thinks that living together is no longer possible. When a marriage or partnership is dissolved externally, there must be grave reasons for this.

Nevertheless, an external separation should never be carried out in strife, but in agreement. Despite the differences of decision, the one should be and remain well-meaning toward the other and never let a lack of help be felt when it is desired.

The one who walks the path to higher ethics and morals, however, may not fall in love from a purely worldly point of view anymore. If he again chooses a life companion, he should follow the criteria of high ethics and morals. These are: Love selflessly and be mindful of your neighbor's inner values. From the very beginning, strive for openness and mutual trust!

If you again choose a life companion, the desire for the physical union should lose its importance. The union should be based on a spiritual friendship or spiritual partnership. It should be based on inner love, and community with God and your neighbor.

A true union does not know sexual *demands*. The love that expresses itself in physical union is a giving-of-oneself-to-the-other and not two bodies working something off.

In a *spiritual partnership* sexuality is not nurtured, but the physical relationship is ennobled. Then the physical union will become a meeting and not a craving. When two people who are aligned with God love each other, they will meet each other from within. If it then comes to physical contact, God is still central to it, despite everything: These people will sense the presence of God's love, and will love each other selflessly and not work something off on each other.

When God is in the center of a marriage or partnership, the physical contact will take place more and more seldom. It gradually dissolves into the selfless, pure love for each other and for God.

So, where God is in the center, marriage and partnership become a deep, close community of life, in which God, our heavenly Father, is the central life. Then both life companions strive to fulfill the commandments of God. They love each other out of the selfless love that never fades away.

And so, when you, with your life companion, make a covenant with God, then you should vow faithfulness, love and trust to each other.

Dear sister, dear brother, later, when the everyday life draws into one's thoughts and life, it is possible that the blissful feelings and vows the two people made to each other in high spirits and happiness at the beginning of their relationship will be forgotten.

In order to be reminded of them again and again and also to admonish oneself, the two life companions should compose a *document of vows* with each other. It can contain the following: The vow that the husband gave to his wife before God and the wife to her husband.

Also the mutual commandments of love for marriage and partnership for a life on earth together should be noted – like, for example, faithfulness, openness, mutual help and selfless love. And any further vows that the husband gives to his wife and the wife to her husband should be entered into the document of vows.

How the partners want to raise their children should also be written down. And so, they should write down who wants to take which responsibilities in love for the child or the children. The document of vows should also lay down how the daily work and duties in the course of the day at home should be shared.

Generally speaking, their life together should be planned, right down to the details of everyday life, in this document of vows

Someone who remains loyal to the vow recognizes that the document of vows is a recurrent theme: It is being with each other and for each other in every situation of life. The one who remains true to his promise before God, whether in marriage or partnership, will gain inner joy, certainty, clarity and an ever deeper spiritual connection with God and with his partner – and beyond this, openness and selfless love toward all people.

A person who composes the document of vows in the spirit of the divine laws for marriage and partnership and remains loyal to these spiritual principles will save himself much sorrow on his spiritual path of evolution. He will still recognize many a karmic tie, but he will not continue weaving on it. A karmic tie that might vibrate toward another person who pleases the man or the woman can, depending on what the cause is, be dissolved by a *friendship*.

The one who keeps to the document of vows, to the covenant with God and his partner, will not add to a possible karma, which he meets in another woman or man. He will not fall in love and, from the state of being in love, do things which could possibly enlarge a still existing correspondence – which could then become a binding for his next life on earth.

The document of vows can be a seal for a life together on earth: Each time when problems arise from everyday life, both partners should look behind the seal, into the document of vows, in order to again orient themselves to what they both promised to each other and to God, their Lord and Father.

The one who, in every difficult situation, reminds himself of the inner values of his companion will be able to prevent many a budding argument with the power of inner love. This could be done through an open conversation or by a gesture of love that shows good will.

Dear brother, dear sister, no matter what life on earth may bring to you and your partner – never neglect either your inner being or your external appearance.

Deep within, every soul longs for beauty, radiance, purity and sublimity and wants to express its inner being also externally.

The content of the spiritual-ethical laws is the inner love that every spirit being in heaven epitomizes. The spiritual-ethical laws encompass beauty, grace, being well-proportioned, gentleness, kindness, earnestness, clarity, openness, and absolute selflessness. They are eternal harmony, sublimity in every spiritual sensation – a consonance of the cosmic powers.

Every spirit being is the Absolute Law. It lives in the fullness and knows no expectations. It rests in itself. This is what the awakened soul within a human being longs deeply for. It takes every chance to give an understanding of these sublime, eternal, spiritual-ethical laws of life to its person. The soul, which strives for purity, for perfection, wants to radiate harmony, sublimity and beauty and to express it through its person.

And so, dear sister, never become careless in your thoughts or in your clothing or your home!

Strive to have great – that is, selfless – thoughts and to retain them. Fight, when human, that is, petty and small-minded, aspects want to overcome you.

A person who thus lives in great thoughts, that is, in deep thoughts of God, will also never neglect his clothing or his home. This does not mean that you should buy clothes that you cannot afford or that you should even live in splendor and luxury. Know that any excess does not serve the sublimity of your awakened soul. On the contrary: Splendor, magnificence and luxury dull the soul and sadden it. Only darkness drapes itself with a lot of gold and jewels and is at ease in luxury, splendor and magnificence – because it lacks the inner light.

But whoever has prepared his soul as a garden of God radiates from within. Accordingly, he will dress harmoniously and cleanly and also live in this manner. A harmonious, clean dress, whose color is in accordance with your light-filled thoughts and life, turns you into a graceful being. With a discreet piece of jewelry, you can accent your radiant inner being, your harmonious gestures and your inner grace.

When your words are also sound and symphony – because they are filled with selflessness – you are a radiant totality that conveys joy to its neighbor without many words.

Know that the way a person thinks is how he radiates. The one who does not rest in himself does not have any great, God-filled thoughts, either. His clothing and his home correspond to this, and this is also how he shows himself to his surroundings.

Dear sister, once you increase the grace and beauty of your inner being, you will also find and address the positive in all that is unlawful. Your husband will continue to love and appreciate you because he feels addressed again and again by the expression of your inner being.

The values of a person are always an expression of his inner power and strength.

A man, too, should never neglect his inner being or his external appearance. The harmony of the inner being brings about the harmony of the external appearance; this expresses itself in and on a person and in the world. Therefore, the radiant male soul, the spiritual positive principle – like the female soul, the spiritual negative principle – never dresses conspicuously, neither in colors nor in shapes. Colors and shapes go together.

The basic attitude of a spiritual man is sincere and open. He radiates strength and protection, that is, secureness. His words are clear and well-balanced. What he says is significant. He is alert and sensitive. He never talks too much or of unimportant things. Therefore, he radiates inner security and spiritual composure. Because his mind is upright, his gait is also upright.

A man on the way to the divine strives to consciously live in God and to speak from the law of God. This is the man who walks toward perfection. He does not have his eye on other women or things. His look is clear and trustworthy. He sees things as they are – not as they seem to be. And just as they are he will tackle and accomplish them.

He is worthy of love but is not a flatterer.

He is enterprising and just in everything he accomplishes. He practices justice before law; this means he will favor the divine law, justice, before the laws of this world. In this way, he will uphold the law with justice wherever it is good for him and his fellowman. Where people are concerned, he will basically consider justice before law. On the other hand, in public matters, where his concerns are not directed against individual people, he will, with the strength of justice, stand up for his rights as a citizen of a state under the rule of law.

He will leave every person his free will and will not oppress him. However, he will address things plainly and clarify them under the law.

He is a faithful life companion to his wife; he protects and respects her and delights in her again and again, when she expresses her awakened soul in great thoughts, selflessness and gracefulness, in words and actions, in clothing and in the home.

A woman should delight in the manliness of her husband, in his external appearance, in his posture and his uprightness, which are emphasized by good, harmonious clothing.

Recognize, dear brother, dear sister, again and again, nature renews its glorious colors and forms. This is why man and woman, the images of God, should also adapt themselves harmoniously to nature through their radiant inner being, their clothing, their movements and gestures.

The external appearance shows what is within: home and clothing – The absoluteness of the heavens – All material things are relative and transient – Everyone needs his own small realm – Outlook for the adolescent: The circle closes – As it is in heaven, similar on earth: extended families in the Kingdom of Peace

The way you think and speak, how you dress and live show who or what has its seat in you.

If your clothes are dirty and you wear glaring colors or ones that don't match, then your home will also be untidy and a jumble of colors.

Your hairdo and your shoes, too, tell who you are and how you live. If your hair is disheveled, if you let it hang unkempt or if it clings to your head and around your shoulders in greasy strings – then in your inner being, too, there will be great chaos and many things will hang and stand around accordingly, in your home. And there will be disorder in your closet as well.

Rundown shoes also indicate an external and internal untidiness – and an unsteady, restless character.

Just as you are, yourself, is how it is in your inner being and in your external appearance, in your apartment or home. As you appear and how you behave toward your fellowman resembles what it looks like in your inner being, in your soul. If your soul is shadowed, if it is dark in you, then you also have gloomy feelings and thoughts.

You will dress and behave according to your sensations and thoughts. And your apartment or house will be in the same condition. If you live with one of your fellowmen and he clears things away for you and puts everything in order – and chooses light and friendly wallpaper and furniture – then it is his consciousness and his radiation, not yours, even if you live in it.

A light-filled soul will transform its home with light, harmoniously matching colors – just as a person, whose spirituality penetrates to without is transformed by God's strength and love. The home of a light-filled person will be bright and friendly.

A few nice accessories, that is, smaller or larger objects, like, for instance, nice, but not necessarily expensive, pictures or paintings, nice vases or candleholders make a home charming and cozy. Remember that colors and shapes bring life into a home and make it enchanting. And so, you recognize that inner spiritual radiation can make many things in the home enchanting.

A light-filled soul does not long for the riches and the splendor of this world; for it has the fullness from God. It knows that as long as it is a human being everything is relative. As a pure spirit being it will live once more among the heavenly colors and forms that are absolute and that absolutely match the nature of the spirit being.

Know that in the divine kingdom everything is absolute. Absolute means: It is perfect – there is no deficiency and no flaw. What awaits you there is divine, that is, absolute.

This will reveal itself in your pure, divine being, in your spiritual clothing, in the spiritual structures, in everything that surrounds you in the divine. This is perfection.

And the homes of the spirit beings are absolute. Their clothing and their homes are an expression of their divinity and their mentality – what they are themselves.

Their true self is their divine nature and thus, an expression of everything that surrounds them. Wherever they move and stop, they personify their nature, their eternal self, their divinity.

It is possible that you could have some difficulty with the terms "self" or "nature": The *self* is the divine being, which is dependent neither on other spirit beings nor on God.

A spirit being has all the forces of the cosmos, the All, as essence in its spiritual body. All the forces of the All serve it. When it addresses the eternal powers in itself, they become active in its spirit body and, at the same time, also in the cosmos, the All. When the All-power in the spiritual body is addressed, it immediately establishes communication with the forces in the All that were addressed.

The spirit being is everything in all things: It is the self, the power in the power and the All in the All.

The *nature*, the mentality, of a spirit being is determined by the plane of heaven in which the spirit being first started to take shape. The spiritual body builds up via the heavenly minerals, plants, animals and nature beings. The forces of mentality, which have developed during the process of evolution from the first spiritual atom to the nature being, increase when the nature being is raised to the filiation of God. They are the spiritual characteristics and the capabilities and aptitudes that result from them.

Know that in the eternal, heavenly homeland there is no standardization of spirit beings: No spirit being is the same as another. The mentality of each spirit being shimmers in a different facet. Just as all-encompassing as the eternal divine law is, are the divine beings, the spirit beings, as well.

When, for example, a spirit being bears within itself many features of the divine Order, it will also have its divine home in one of the planes of heaven of Order. Each of the seven basic levels is contained in every other as a sub-region. And so, for example, the level of Order is contained in all the other basic levels as a sub-region.

According to the light-power that is its nature, the spirit being will dress, create and arrange its home and be active accordingly in infinity. Therefore, no plane of heaven resembles another and no home planet another.

The spiritual planets, the dwelling planets for the divine beings, correspond in their radiation and their shape – you could also say in the landscaping and nature design – to their respective plane of heaven, either to the plane of heaven of Order, of Will, of Wisdom, of Earnestness, of Patience, of Love, or of Mercy. Each basic level – also called heavenly sphere – is contained as a sub-level, as revealed, in each one of the seven basic heavens.

The center of all Being, the *Sanctum of God*, our heavenly Father-Mother-God, is the highest radiation. Its design is unique and fully different than the seven times seven planes of heaven, which revolve around the Sanctum, the seat of God-Father.

When I talk about the Sanctum of God, our Father, I mean the eternal, gold-radiating city of Jerusalem, the center of the universe.

Know that the earth is matter and a tiny spot in the universe. The shape and design of its external appearance is only a pale reflection of the eternally existing home – just like the clothing and the homes of people correspond to their level of development.

190

Therefore, everything material, the life on earth and everything created on earth is merely relative and never absolute. Everything relative is subject to constant change and is therefore also transient.

The world – and with this I mean what happens on earth – corresponds to the condition of the light-filled or shadowed souls and thus, to the respective feelings and thoughts of the individual persons. This is why clothing, hairstyle, shoes, one's life style and the interior arrangement of homes are constantly changing.

Everything that happens on earth corresponds to the level of evolution of the people. Evolution means development. Someone who develops spiritually changes from within as a human being. Just as a person's feelings, thoughts, words and actions change – in a positive sense toward higher ethics and morals as well as in a negative sense right up to amorality – so will his clothing and the furnishings of his apartment or house change accordingly.

If the soul is shadowed, the person will be careless about his external appearance or he will drape himself with all kinds of valuable things; he might also arrange his apartment or house accordingly. If he has money and possessions, he may – depending on how and with what his soul is burdened – convert them into magnificence and splendor and decorate his apartment or house with expensive things.

But when from the soul of a materially rich person – who considers his money and possessions as his own – the internal poverty breaks through, the milieu of his soul is a radiating morass. He then lives and moves in this, also externally. He will cling to whatever money or possessions he still has, like a drowning person wanting to cling to a straw.

The one who is not of this world, that is, who strives for what is spiritual and ethical, for the fine and pure, will also live nicely and harmoniously, but not in splendor and luxury. The spiritual-ethical person will live on an upper middle-class level.

People of the Spirit will arrange their earthly home nicely and harmoniously. They will also dress harmoniously and neatly. However, they do not live in splendor and luxury, nor do they wear expensive and sumptuous clothes and adorn themselves with expensive jewelry.

The one who has brought his self to unfoldment radiates from within, even without any external attributes. Every person radiates what he is: pure spirituality or impure humanness or both mixed together. This is also why each person is on a different level of consciousness. The soul of the person is imprinted by its former lives and radiates purity as well as those things that have not been cleared up. A person is also shaped by his parents' house: he dresses and creates his own home accordingly.

This is why every person should have a room of his own which he furnishes and arranges the way he feels at the moment – the way he would like to furnish and arrange it, right now. When a person changes in his way of thinking and living, in his consciousness, his clothing and his home will also change.

One's own small realm, for example, one's own room, should also be kept when you enter a marriage or partnership. Even if two people love each other very much and both have made a covenant with God together, each one of them should still be surrounded by his own, personal aura.

The aura of a home consists of the radiation and the colors of the furniture and curtains. It develops from pictures and from the many little objects that the inhabitant has placed in a certain spot, so they catch his eye again and again and he can delight in them.

The sleeping area, too, should not be shared. At night, that is, from going to bed until the next morning, the lovers should not sleep in the same room. From a spiritual point of view, one can say the following: When long term, that is, for a longer period of time, two people share a bedroom together, then at night their souls cannot always hover unimpeded in those spheres to which they could travel according to their intensity of light – when their bodies lie in deep sleep.

For better understanding, please note: At night when the soul leaves the body – when the person is fast asleep – the watchful soul and the person's guardian spirit are always on the alert, so that the soul can return in time *before* the person awakes.

When a disturbance causes the body to awaken with a jerk and if it happens again and again, it can trigger problems in the person, because the soul cannot securely anchor itself in the body in time, or can take the journey into higher spheres of life less and less frequently. It will then always remain close to the sleeping body.

If, for example, two people share a bedroom and one of them sleeps very restlessly, because he had many difficulties and problems that day – be it with himself or with his neighbor – then his soul cannot withdraw very far from his body. The other sleeper who could have slept well will be disturbed and awakened by this restlessness. This means that his soul, too, cannot withdraw very far from his body.

I repeat: when one of the partners sleeps restlessly, the guardian spirit of the *other one* has to be on the lookout, because its protégé is often disturbed by the restlessness of his partner and therefore cannot fall into deep sleep and his soul cannot go to higher regions.

If such disturbances occur quite often, then both partners lose life energy, because at night both souls are unable to withdraw further from their restlessly sleeping bodies. And so, it is less and less frequently that their souls reach higher, light-filled regions of energy, in order to receive life energy there for soul and body. This is why the life force, the vibration of both souls, diminishes and thus, at the same time, the life energy of the bodies.

Indications for this are: The person looses vigor and vitality; already in the morning he is tired, listless and has not slept enough – or negative thoughts attack him already upon awakening; or problems bother him that he thought were already cleared up. Such and similar symptoms indicate that at night, the soul could not go where it could receive light and strength.

If it is blocked in this way over and over again because of the person's behavior, this will also affect him, resulting in annoyance and stress. The consequence can be that dissension arises between the two partners. These then also affect the family and the domestic peace is disturbed.

These emotional pressures also affect the course of the person's day and his activities. His occupational development can also be disturbed. The togetherness which began as selfless love may also be harmed by such unconscious occurrences.

Even when both really love each other, each partner still has his own mentality and human habits. For example, one is very tired in the evening and would like to fall sleep right away, while the other one might like to read in bed for a while or listen to some music. If the light or the music bothers the other one, the partner who still wants to read or listen to the radio will respect the other one and turn out the light. But for how long will this work out well?

Every person should have the chance to develop! And for this he needs his own small realm, not at all a palace or a large apartment. It can be, as already revealed, a nicely arranged living room-bedroom within an apartment.

You can retreat to this, your own small realm, when you wish to be alone, to pray or to meditate, to read or listen to music. Then you do not disturb your neighbor who at the same time might like to pursue other interests.

When you also sleep in your own small realm at night, you are embedded in your vibration. Nothing and nobody disturbs you – unless you disturb yourself because during the day you acted unlawfully, overreacting or parting in quarrel from your fellowman.

If you take negative thoughts, for example, about the events of the day or about all the things you have not yet cleared up, along to your room, you will be troubled by your own vibrations and sleep restlessly at night. Then it is *because of you* that your soul cannot go to more light-filled regions, because your consciousness, your conscience, troubles you; for you have done or said something that was not in accordance with Order. But you will not hold back your neighbor's soul!

When you have your own small realm, you can, at any time, also think over difficulties and problems that still bother you or which are still unsolved, without disturbing your neighbor.

So, it is not a problem when you turn on the light to note down what you have realized or what you plan for the next day; or you can pray aloud, listen to soft music or pick up reading material that helps you calm down again. And you will not disturb your partner.

Furthermore, recognize that each person has a different rhythm of the day. When he can let it end in his own small realm, he will feel strengthened to meet the new day and begin it joyfully.

The small living-and-sleeping-areas of the partners shall not indicate that they have separated. On the contrary! They shall come together at the right time and at the right hour; for being with each other and for each other are particularly necessary, so that love and openness toward each other are nurtured in a marriage or partnership.

Wherever people live together, in marriage, partnership or family, there should be a *common* living room. And people in living communities, where singles, married couples or partners come together, should arrange a common living room. This room should be arranged by all members of the living community in a warm and comfortable way so that everyone feels good there.

So, it is recommended that each one have a small realm of his own that he can arrange according to his inner being and to his external ideas.

Not everything you like now has to stay like this forever. Just like a person changes he will also change his clothes and his home. Know that the wallpaper, colors, shapes and objects you like today might not correspond to you anymore after some time. Note well: I used the word "correspond"! So, what you like today is an expression of your present level of development. It is possible that after some time you will like other colors and shapes. Also the objects with which you have decorated your apartment or your room – even if they are tiny little things – will then no longer correspond to your nature, to your radiation.

You are quite right when you now say: I can't keep buying new things all the time! This is correctly thought. That is why you should not buy things that are too expensive!

And if you do have expensive furniture, then just change the wallpaper, for example, and rearrange the furniture. Purchase a nice bowl or other small ornaments. Also new curtains or a nice rug can transform the room.

My advice to all people striding forward on the Inner Path toward God – that is, who want to spiritually develop – would be to establish a secondhand market with objects of an upper quality of life. There, many things can certainly be found that are reasonably priced. Someone gives something away for a reasonable price because he was able to buy something else that now appeals to him more. His neighbor can then buy it at a reasonable price and delights in it because it corresponds to his present nature.

This does not mean that only those people who are developing give away their things. Often a person inherits wonderful furniture but it does not correspond to his vibration. And so, he gives it away. It is also possible that the parents or grandparents had a higher vibration than their heir.

Sometimes people fall back to their previous level of consciousness, because a karma came to them that they did not want to overcome, but to live it out and enjoy it. Things that used to be dear to them now do not interest them anymore and they give them away – for their interest has found another point of reference. Thus, when people fall back into an earthly way of life and do not want to be reminded of their past – perhaps spiritual – life, they then dispose of what could, for example, trigger their conscience.

On the way toward the divine consciousness, steps backward are also possible. Such people give in to their karma, the causes that are flowing out, and prefer whatever now corresponds to their thoughts and their life.

We do not want to encourage going backward on the Inner Path; this should only be a hint for you. If you experience that people fall back into the material way of life again, do not try to hold them back with many words and a lot of advice. Explain and pray! Every person, even if he falls back or stagnates, will find his spiritual basis again sooner or later, and build upon it anew. However, it can then be a very arduous path.

And so, you can see that on the path of evolution, a person changes his way of thinking and acting – and with it, his clothing and his home.

Dear brother, dear sister, when children emerge from your marriage or partnership, strive to set up a small realm of their own for them.

During the first days or weeks, the little darling depends fully on its mother or father and sleeps in its mother's room or father's room. But from the first hours of its earthly existence, it should have its own little bed.

With the child's first cry, the soul starts to radiate the soul programs it brought along via the physical body it has taken – that is, via the baby. Right after birth, the baby already has its own radiation. Nevertheless, the soul will only gradually become able to cope with its body in order to be able to unfold and to learn to master the five senses.

This is why it is important that soul and baby have a lot of peace and quiet. If the little earth-citizen were to sleep in its parent's bed, it would gradually affect him just as it does his parents when they share a bedroom at night: The soul of the little earth-citizen would be exposed to several different vibrations again and again and would not have the peace it needs to get the senses of its physical body under control. Likewise, the soul's journey to faraway regions would be interrupted over and over again.

Once their baby has thrived to the extent that mother and father can put the crib into the child's room without worrying, they should do so! The baby's soul will thank them. It will meet its body, its earthly garment, more freely, because it brings much light and strength from its nightly journey to other worlds.

The negative vibrations of its father or mother, in which problems and desires can vibrate, do not disturb the little body, but disturbs the soul, which is endeavoring to get its body under control for this earthly existence. But when the baby sleeps in its own small realm, the soul is not hindered from going to those worlds where it came from or where it still has to master some things at night.

If a family has several children and two or even three of them sleep in one room, the children also disturb each other! This happens as I have already revealed: The souls of the children cannot go to other worlds without being disturbed. The restlessness of one child disturbs the other one or ones, so that spiritual development at night is hardly possible because the souls cannot go to where they would receive – according to their spiritual development – strength and love, in order to pass it on to their physical bodies.

Quarrelling and fighting among the little brothers and sisters often arise because they sleep together and their souls therefore can convey little energy to their bodies, since they have to remain close to their sleeping bodies. For this reason, it would be good for the development of the children if each one could have its own small realm.

As soon as the child has developed the ability to differentiate between colors and shapes, it should arrange its own small realm itself, with the help of its parents. The soul will choose via the child which colors and shapes the child needs so it can delight in them and be happy. Happiness, love and joy bring about harmony in soul and person.

Healthy growth and thriving is possible for a child only when it is in harmony. Then the soul of the child feels well and strives to convey to the body, its person, the divine impulses that are active in it.

Its favorite toys – for example, its favorite stuffed animals or a doll, which are small living creatures for the child, with which it is in close contact – help the child to gradually grow into a harmonious interaction of the cosmic forces. For the child comes into communication with the fine, harmonious forces of nature by way of its stuffed animals.

When a child has a harmonious connection to its doll, its teddy, to the cat or any other little stuffed animal, it is possible for its guardian spirit to now and then call the child's attention to something or to guide it via its favorite toy. In this way, the guardian spirit can establish a closer contact to the child through its favorite doll, for instance. For example, when the child dresses the doll and puts it in a certain place, then, by the appearance and posture of the doll or by the way it is dressed, the guardian spirit can awaken positive sensations or thoughts in the child, which help it to mature spiritually.

In the book "I Tell a Story – Are You Listening?" for children from six to twelve years of age, you can read more about the favorite toys, like the doll, the teddy or cat.

Dear sister, dear brother, take the following axiom deep into yourself and let it become a guiding thought for you:

You and your neighbor mature in the stillness. Find stillness within yourself first, and live in such a way that you do not give your neighbor reason to justly get angry with you.

In deep stillness, soul and person find their way to God. In deep stillness, two people can also find each other for a life on earth.

This does not mean that you should avoid your fellowman, on the contrary. You have already heard that your neighbor can be a mirror for you! But in order to find inner stillness, you should be able to retreat to your own small realm, so that soul and body can gather strength for the following hours of the day or for the new day.

Dear sister, dear brother, the circle closes:

Once your parents told their children or their child, that is, you, about the spiritual life.

Through the eternal truth, from which I, Liobani, was privileged to convey spiritual principles to the parents and children of this earth, via the prophetess and messenger of God – from the first day of life to twelve years of age – parents gained insight into the spiritual life and into the feelings, thoughts and wants of their child or their children, also into their joys, fears and worries.

During spiritual games, the parents gained insight into the inner life of their children, thus experiencing their children as they are – and not as they act. Through favorite playmates, such as a cat, a teddy or a doll, as well as through drawings, the parents were able to grasp what their children think about and what moves them unconsciously. They learned about the deep fears and troubles of their child or children, as well as their light-filled sides, their joys, their selfless affection and love; and they experienced the children's happiness.

All of this moved the parents to keep a book of insights or a book of life for their children. In it, they conscientiously noted everything important and through this, gained insight and an overview of the highs and lows of their children. And they learned and recognized from this how to approach their children and what they, themselves, should keep in mind, in order to become good friends to their children.

Especially through playmates like a cat, teddy or doll, the parents gained insight again and again into the wishes and longings of their children; for children often unconsciously tell their small or big troubles to their favorite toys. Thereby, parents often have to experience that their children have created a deeper connection to the cat, the teddy or doll than to them – because the favorite toys kept quiet and patiently listened to what the child had to tell them.

From all this, the parents could recognize the child's aptitudes, its abilities, talents and qualities. Much of it is recorded in the book of insights, the child's book of life.

Now you have become a father or a mother yourself. If your parents kept a book of insights for you and you conscientiously kept your journal from your 12th birthday on, and now keep the book of vows, then you have your entire development in hand: from the day of your birth on earth to the day your first child is born.

And when you do likewise for your children as your parents have done for you, then, one day, you, too, can give a great treasure to your children, not only through a selfless guidance, but also through the record of their path through life.

And so, when you conscientiously consider everything that God, the Father of us all, revealed through me, Liobani, you will be able to stand by your child in many situations of life and recognize it in the depths of its nature.

In heaven all spirit beings are brothers and sisters because they all have *one* Father, who, through His Spirit, is also Mother to them. The love-radiation of God for His children is the Father-Mother-radiation of the Father-Mother-Principle; it is also called the *Father-Mother-God.*

Although all spirit beings are brothers and sisters, they still form families. The primordial Father-Mother-Principle is God; the manifestation is also called *Primordial Father* or *Father-Ur.* All children of God emerged and emerge from the Father-Mother-Principle. When in and about them all the laws of infinity are developed, they enter into a union of duality. On earth, the union of two people is called marriage or partnership.

In the eternal Being, the union of two spirit beings, a positive and a negative principle, which means a male and a female principle, is called a *dual union.*

This dual union holds true for all of eternity, because in the eternal Being everything is absolute, that is, perfect. In the dual love there is no vacillation. The dual couple love each other in the same way forever.

From the dual love *spirit children* develop which, in turn, are the children of God, because God, the all-eternal law of love, brings forth everything that exists.

So out of the dual union a *spiritual family* develops. From it, emerges the spiritual tree of life – you could also call it a spiritual family tree which, as a whole, includes the *spiritual clan*. The many families that emerged from an ancestral family and form a clan as a whole are pure spirit beings, children of God. So, there are many families and clans in the divine kingdom. All families of heaven together form *one* large family in God – because all of them are children of God.

The Father-Mother-God is the Primordial-Father-Mother-Principle. The dual father and the dual mother form the dual couple. God, the Primordial-Father-Mother-Principle, gives the filiation of God to further children via the dual couple.

When people live together in peace and harmony, they bring heaven to earth, then, they think, live and act *similarly* to the pure beings in heaven.

As I have already revealed, in the three-dimensional world, on earth, everything is relative. Therefore, I used and use the word "similar." As long as the earth exists, everything will be merely relative, only similar to heaven; nothing will be absolute.

But the thinking, living and acting of the children of God in the earthly garment should be similar as in heaven!

God, our Father – the Primordial-Father-Mother-Principle – wants all of His earthly children to draw closer to the divine, to their true being, again. This is why Christ, the Redeemer of all people and souls, revealed that the Kingdom of God, the Kingdom of Peace, will come to the earth.

In the World Kingdom of Jesus Christ, the Kingdom of Peace, it shall be similar on earth as it is in heaven: Families shall join together to form extended families.

In the extended families the women should not be the so-called little housewife at the stove, but assume duties in the community according to her attributes and abilities, thus working with the men, their brothers. Then the woman, too, can also contribute with her attributes, abilities, talents and qualities, in order to wholly take part in the life of the Kingdom of Peace of Jesus Christ.

The women, the sisters, will alternately take care of home and the children in the extended family; this means that for certain days or hours they are responsible for the domestic duties like cleaning, laundry, cooking and baking.

If there is already a dining house for the members of the community where the community of the Lord can partake together of the gifts of God, the food, then the effort of cooking and baking can be significantly reduced.

For the children there is the Father-Mother-House where they are taken care of for one or several days. Grandparents can also take on this duty of love for the little ones!

In the Father-Mother-House for children up to the age of twelve, or perhaps beyond that, they are given everything they need for their spiritual and physical development. In the Father-Mother-House, the Spirit of the Primordial-Father-Mother-Principal shall be effective: the selfless love for all children, without exception – no matter whether a child behaves well or another one is difficult.

Once these and other facilities are established on earth, more and more people will join in the Spirit of God – consciously as inhabitants of the Kingdom of Peace of Jesus Christ.

Dear sister, dear brother, the Kingdom of Peace, the World Kingdom of Jesus Christ is emerging. You, too should be an inhabitant of the Kingdom of God on earth.

More and more people are working for the Kingdom of Peace of Jesus Christ on earth by deciding for Christ.

I, Liobani, was also able to give a small contribution from the eternal kingdom for the Kingdom of Peace of Jesus Christ on earth. Gratefully, I bow before the All-Highest, whose daughter I am.

Vivified by the inner, selfless love and filled with joy over the fact that many children, young people and adults are hearing the call of the Lord through His prophetess and messenger and are walking the path of selfless love – and also finding the truth in the books by "Liobani" and actualizing it – I take my leave of my brothers and sisters in the earthly garment with the words:

I am linked with you throughout eternity.

Peace, my dear brothers and my dear sisters in the earthly garment,

Liobani